Credits

D1373446

Authors

Derrin Michael Kent

Richard William Hand

Glenys Gillian Bradbury

Margaret Anne Kent

Reviewers

Alex Büchner

Heinz Krettek

Nigel McNie

Acquisition Editor

David Barnes

Development Editor

Ved Prakash Jha

Technical Editors

Bhupali Khule

Vinodhan Nair

Gaurav Datar

Mithun Sehgal

Conrad Neil Sardinha

Editorial Team Leader

Abhijeet Deobhakta

Indexer

Hemangini Bari

Project Team Leader

Lata Basantani

Project Coordinator

Rajashree Hamine

Proofreader

Chris Smith

Production Coordinators

Shantanu Zagade

Aparna Bhagat

Cover Work

Shantanu Zagade

Aparna Bhagat

About the Authors

Derrin Kent (http://derr.in) graduated in Education Studies in 1988 and has worked in the Education Sector in the UK and Overseas ever since, gaining a Master's Level Diploma in Adult Teaching from the University of Cambridge in 1995. Derrin has been an amateur website designer for over 10 years and has worked with Moodle since version 1.5. Derrin has already worked as the Technical Reviewer for two books on Moodle published by Packt.

A big Linux fanboy, Derrin set up an open-source software hosting, configuring, and training business (http://tdm.info) in 2007 and qualified formally as a Linux-Certified Professional in 2008.

TDM became the second official Mahara Partner Organization in the UK in 2008 and now professionally host, configure, and train both end users (learners) and software administrators (geeks) to work with Mahara sites.

Derrin believes strongly in the value of social-constructionist learning approaches and is a committed advocate of learner-owned data and of Portfolio-based learning approaches.

Derrin speaks Spanish at home with his beautiful Peruvian wife, Ely, and his two wonderful bilingual kids, Salvador and Micaela.

Thanks to all three of you for your patience with me and my work-life imbalance, and thanks also to the TDM Team for the same.

Richard Hand is a Mahara platform manager, module developer, and theme/configuration designer for TDM (`http://tdm.info`). Richard also supports and develops for other open-source software platforms including Moodle, Drupal, and Joomla. He graduated with a first class honors degree in Computer Science from the University of Bristol in 2008 and won a national (UK) award for "Best Website Design" for one of his TDM Joomla sites in 2009 (selected from 2000+ competitor sites).

I would like to thank David Hoyos for all the work he put into the illustrations for this book.

Glenys Bradbury is a Cambridge University graduate and is now a Prince2-qualified Project Manager and an LSIS E-guide who works as a Mahara (and Moodle) learning-designer, site-administrator, and end-user trainer for TDM (`http://tdm.info`). Glen has extensive working experience as a trainer and manager in both educational and business environments. She is a friendly and sensitive change-manager who really knows how to make a personal development planning / knowledge management implementation process come to life.

Meg Kent has worked continuously as a corporate manager and director in a variety of Work-Based Learning contexts since the late 1980s. She is now a Mahara (and Moodle) learning-designer and end-user trainer for TDM (`http://tdm.info`). Also a Work-Based Learning assessor in her own right, Meg successfully blends support for individuals' achievement of government-funded qualifications alongside the development of their practical Web 2.0 skills.

About the Reviewers

Alex Büchner is the co-founder and technical lead of Synergy Learning (www.synergy-learning.com), the UK's leading Moodle and Mahara partner. He has been working with ePortfolio systems and virtual learning environments of all shapes and sizes since their advent on the educational landscape. Services offered include Mahara and Moodle hosting, support, training, and branding.

Alex holds a PhD in Computer Science and an MSc in Software Engineering. He has authored over 50 international publications, including *Moodle Administration* published by Packt Publishing, and is a frequent speaker on Moodle, Mahara, and related open-source technologies.

Nigel McNie began his career in free software when he was just 17, working part time as an intern at Catalyst IT. His first contribution to the free software world was the popular GeSHi syntax highlighter, which can be found to this day highlighting source code on sites such as Wikipedia. In 2005, he dropped out of university to work full time, and began on the Mahara project in 2006. Now, Nigel leads development on the project, and has designed and co-written large parts of the codebase, including the Views framework and LEAP2A support.

Catalyst IT has been a top place to work these last few years. I know few companies that trust their developers so much to do the right thing, nor who understand the benefits of free software. Keep up the good fight, guys.

I would like to thank my fellow developers for all the time, sweat, and blood that have gone into Mahara currently, and for supporting me in rough times – in particular, Penny Leach and Richard Mansfield. You guys believe in Mahara, and as a result routinely go beyond the call.

Finally, thanks to the Mahara community: contributors to `mahara.org`, partners, right through to Richard Wyles at the top. You guys are amazing. You buy into the vision for Mahara, and are putting in the hard yards to make it happen. Wherever you are, I owe you a beer. Especially if you're running Mahara on PostgreSQL.

Heinz Krettek is a German teacher at a school for vocational education. He studied business sciences and sports. His main job is to prepare socioeconomically deprived students for lifelong learning. In 2006 he discovered the portfolio work and began to translate the German langpack for Mahara. The first translations for Mahara 0.6 were published on his own Moodle site. Soon after Nigel McNie installed a git repository the actual files were published in the Mahara git.

He organized several education and training sessions for teachers and was speaker at the German moodlemoots. Since 2008 Heinz has been partner of a company that offers LMS hosting and Mahara hosting. His company is the official German Mahara Partner.

He lives with his wife and the four kids in the Black Forest. In his spare time Heinz prefers the 3 M's: Mahara, Moodle, and marathon. He finished the New York Marathon. His motto is: who finished a marathon will struggle all problems in school ;-)

Table of Contents

Preface	**1**
Chapter 1: What Can Mahara Do for Me?	**7**
Portfolios go electronic	8
Towards an ePortfolio-enabled future	9
Ways of using Mahara	9
Case study one: Punam from Pennytown Primary	10
Case study two: Janet Norman from Pharmaceuticals International Inc. (PI Inc.)	11
Case study three: Neil from Training 4 Work	13
Time for action – looking at some real-life Maharas	14
Why Mahara?	15
Personalized learning	16
Reflective learning	17
Collaborative learning	18
Join the Mahara community	20
Time for action – registering and exploring further	22
Summary	26
Chapter 2: Getting Started with Mahara	**27**
Registering with a Mahara site	27
Time for action – registering onto the demonstration site	28
Logging in for the first time	30
Time for action – logging in	30
Mahara's user interface—finding your way around	31
A word on Mahara themes	31
The main menu and submenus	32
Site blocks	33
The footer	33

Setting up your own profile   **33**

Profile information   34

Editing your profile   34

Time for action – editing your profile   **34**

Profile icons   36

Time for action – uploading your profile icons   **37**

Editing your resumé goals and skills   38

Time for action – editing your resumé goals and skills   **39**

Your profile page   **41**

Time for action – viewing and investigating your profile page   **41**

The profile page wall   43

Some more profile page examples   43

Adding a text box to your profile page   **44**

Time for action – creating a text box for your profile page   **45**

Options in the text editor   48

Time for action – editing a text box by adding a hyperlink   **48**

Taking the formatting and editing one step further   50

Time for action – adding an image to your text box   **51**

Summary   **52**

Chapter 3: Add Files and Blogs to Your Portfolio   **53**

Putting your files online   **53**

Mahara replaces the USB stick   53

Time for action – adding some folders and files to your Portfolio   **54**

Giving structure to your folder tree and branches   56

Copyright   56

Upload limit   57

Moving and deleting files   57

Uploading more than one file   58

Time for action – multiple file upload   **58**

Using tagging to organize your files and search for them   59

Blogging   **62**

What is a blog?   62

Time for action – creating your first Mahara blog   **63**

Embedding an image in your blog post   66

Linking to files, folders, and blogs in your Profile Page   **68**

Time for action – linking to files, folders, and blogs in your Profile Page   **68**

Summary   **72**

Chapter 4: Views   **73**

What are Views in Mahara?   **73**

Time for action – creating and laying out your View   **75**

Adding/removing columns from your View	79
Time for action – changing your View layout	80
Time for action – adding View details	82
View access	83
Time for action – editing your View access	83
Making a View copyable	85
Deciding who can access your View	86
Time-limiting access	88
Editing your View once you have created it	89
Blocks	90
Copying Views	93
Time for action – copying a View	94
View feedback	96
Time for action – feedback on a View's content	96
Best practice example – multi-page view	99
Time for action – linking Views together to make a multi-page View	100
Assessing the quality of your View	102
View quality checklist	103
Aesthetics	103
Content	104
Summary	106
Chapter 5: Working in Groups and Interacting with Friends	**107**
Groups	107
Time for action – creating a group	108
Group types	110
Open membership groups	110
Request membership groups	111
Invite only groups	111
Navigating your new group	112
Time for action – opening up and navigating around your group	112
The groups shortcut sideblock	114
Joining an open membership group	115
Time for action – joining a group in maharaforbeginners.tdm.info	115
Managing your group members	116
Time for action – removing group members and changing roles	116
Group forums	119
Time for action – creating a forum	120
Forum moderation	122
Managing your forum	123

The exciting bit: Forum topics   **124**
  Forum discussion frameworks   125
Time for action – adding a discussion topic   **126**
Naming forums and their topic subjects   **129**
Posting to a topic   **129**
Time for action – replying to a topic post   **130**
Group files   **132**
Group views   **133**
Finding Groups   **134**
Time for action – finding and joining a group   **135**
Joining a request membership group   **136**
Time for action – requesting to join a group   **137**
Accepting/Denying requests to join a group   **138**
Making friends!   **138**
Time for action – finding friends and adding them to your list   **139**
Responding to a friend request   **140**
Managing your friends   **140**
Time for action – filtering and removing friends   **140**
Summary   **142**

Chapter 6: Site Settings and Exporting Your Portfolio   **143**
Preferences   **144**
Time for action – changing your preferences   **144**
  Changing username and password   145
  Friends control   146
  HTML editor   146
  Messages from other users   146
  Show controls to add and remove columns when editing a view   147
  Maximum tags in cloud   148
Preferences in the right sidebar   **148**
Notifications   **148**
Time for action – managing your notifications   **149**
Watchlist   **152**
Activity preferences   **152**
Time for action – choosing your activity preferences   **153**
Exporting your portfolio   **157**
Time for action – exporting your portfolio   **157**
  HTML website export   160
  LEAP2A export   160
Summary   **161**

Chapter 7: Institution Administrators, Staff Members, and Group Tutors   163

What is an institution?   164

  Administering an institution   165

Time for action – adding users to your institution   166

Bulk uploading users to your institution   169

Time for action – adding institutional users by CSV   169

Editing user account settings   171

Time for action – finding a user and suspending them   172

Masquerading as another user   173

Managing member roles in your institution   175

Time for action – managing your institution's members, staff and admins   175

Configuring your institution's settings   177

Dealing with admin notifications   178

Institution views and files   179

  Views   179

  Files   180

Less learner-driven aspects of Mahara   181

What is a course group?   182

  Case study   185

Time for action – setting up a Course: Controlled Membership group   185

Publicly viewable groups   186

Tutors   187

Time for action – adding a Tutor to your course group   188

Submitting work for assessment   190

Time for action – submitting a view to a course group for assessment   190

Time for action – releasing a view submitted for assessment   192

Putting it all together into an assessment process   193

Time for action – an example assessment process with Mahara   195

Summary   198

Appendix A: Mahara Implementation Pre-Planner   199

What's involved with a Mahara implementation?   201

Analysis and Specification   202

  Deciding if Mahara is right for you   202

  Understanding your own specific needs and working conditions   206

    Concept 1: Purpose   208

    Concept 2: Learning Activity Design   208

    Concept 3: Processes   208

    Concept 4: Ownership   209

    Concept 5: Disruptive Nature   209

Choosing between a Mahara partner-supported site or your own installation   209
Scoping out your implementation plan   209
    Decide on your implementation timeframe   210
    Ensure you have the people's commitment   210
    Draft out your initial Mahara design   210
    Draft out your Mahara-specific policies   212
    Start to embed Mahara into institutional and program priorities   213
Design and implementation   **213**
Creating a buzz!   213
Getting some quick wins in first!   214
Continuously involving your users in the design process   215
Keep going despite adversity!   215
Evaluation and continuation   **217**
Reviewing and re-evaluating   218
Changing and embedding   219
Appendix B: Installing Mahara   **221**
What will you need?   **221**
Downloading Mahara   **222**
Time for action – downloading Mahara   **222**
Using the command line   **223**
Time for action – creating your Mahara file structure   **224**
Creating the database   **224**
Time for action – creating the Mahara database   **225**
Setting up the data directory   **226**
Time for action – setting up the data directory   **226**
Time for action – creating the config.php file   **227**
Running the Installer   **228**
Time for action – running the installer   **229**
The last step: Setting up a cron process   **229**
Can I install Mahara on Windows?   230
What about installation on other operating systems?   230
What is a Mahara partner and what can they do for me?   **230**
Finding a Mahara partner   231

Appendix C: Pop Quiz Answers   233
Chapter 2   233
Understanding your profile information   233
Chapter 3   233
files, folders, and tagging   233
blogging in Mahara   233
Chapter 4   234
Creating a View   234
Copying Views   234
Chapter 5   234
Creating Mahara Groups   234
Group Forums   235
Chapter 6   235
Activity Types   235
Export   235
Chapter 7   235
Managing an Institution   235

Index   237

Preface

Mahara is a user-centered environment with a permission framework that enables different views of an ePortfolio to be easily managed. These views help you display your artefacts in a way you choose and to the people you want. You can also create online communities and social networks through groups, blogs, and forums.

Being a new user, you will need a quick and easy implementation guide to set up your feature-rich digital portfolio.

This is your step-by-step guide to building your own impressive educational or professional ePortfolio using Mahara. The book covers the key features of Mahara that will help you set up your customized digital portfolio and display your own stuff in your chosen way allowing contribution from selected users only.

This book will introduce you to the exciting features of the Mahara framework and help you develop a feature-rich ePortfolio for yourself. You will see how easily you can upload multiple files like journals, project documents, pictures, or videos, and share them with your friends. You will also learn to set up views of these files in easy-to-create web pages, making these visible to your chosen ones only, and learn to allow people to give their inputs.

You will learn to create blogs and forums and get connected to the rest of the world. Imagine how good you will feel when you see your knowledge, success, and ideas going live and available to your chosen audiences. This book is for you—go grab it!

What this book covers

Chapter 1, *What can Mahara do for me?*, we look at what an ePortfolio essentially is and the possible uses of Mahara. We also look at some real-life Mahara sites and learn what is so special about the Mahara ePortfolio.

Chapter 2, *Getting Started with Mahara*, looks at how to register onto a demonstration Mahara site, logging in, and navigating around Mahara. We also look at creating our own profile page and using the Mahara text editor.

Chapter 3, *Add Files and Blogs to Your Portfolio*, we look at how to add files, folders, and blogs to our Portfolio. We will also learn about how to tag things in our Portfolio.

Chapter 4, *Views*, covers how to create and edit a View, as well as controlling who sees the View and when they see it.

Chapter 5, *Working in Groups and Interacting with Friends*, we will cover creating groups, discussing Group Types, Forums and discussions, Group Views and Files, and making friends.

Chapter 6, *Site Settings and Exporting Your Portfolio*, looks at setting our preferences, managing our notifications, the watchlist, adjusting our activity preferences, and exporting our portfolio.

Chapter 7, *Institution Administrators, Staff Members, and Group Tutors*, covers roles that an Institutional Administrator performs. We will also look at a special type of Group called a Course Group and the two types of roles associated with it.

Appendix A, *Mahara Implementation Pre-Planner*, we will discuss some of the important questions and suggestions your organization will need to address, if you want to quickly and successfully get your ePortfolio system up, live and running.

Appendix B, *Installing Mahara*, covers the installation of Mahara, along with the requirements for installation.

Appendix C, *Pop Quiz Answers*, contains the answers for the pop quiz questions.

What you need for this book

All you will need to get started with this book is access to the internet via a web browser. You will be able to use the demonstration Mahara to go through the examples in the book (http://maharaforbeginners.tdm.info) but it would be a useful if you had your own Mahara website in operation too (see *Appendix B* for installation details).

Who this book is for

This book is for learners who want to maintain online documentation of their projects and share it with a particular teacher or trainer for feedback, educators who want to set up an ePortfolio for their students in order to encourage and advance personalized and reflective learning, or professionals who want to share journals and project documents with their team, capturing and sharing their existing knowledge and creating new knowledge in communities of professional practice.

Conventions

In this book, you will find several headings appearing frequently.

To give clear instructions of how to complete a procedure or task, we use:

Time for action – Heading

1. Action 1

2. Action 2

3. Action 3

Instructions often need some extra explanation so that they make sense, so they are followed by:

What Just Happened?

This section explains the working of tasks or instructions that you have just completed.

You will also find some other learning aids in the book, including:

Pop quiz – Heading

These are short multiple choice questions intended to help you test your own understanding.

Have a go hero – Heading

These set practical challenges and give you ideas for experimenting with what you have learned.

You will also find a number of styles of text that distinguish between different kinds of information. Here are some examples of these styles, and an explanation of their meaning.

Code words in text are shown as follows: "We can include other contexts through the use of the `include` directive."

New terms and **important words** are shown in bold. Words that you see on the screen, in menus or dialog boxes for example, appear in the text like this: "clicking the **Next** button moves you to the next screen".

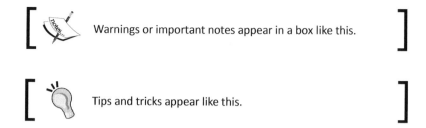

Warnings or important notes appear in a box like this.

Tips and tricks appear like this.

Reader feedback

Feedback from our readers is always welcome. Let us know what you think about this book—what you liked or may have disliked. Reader feedback is important for us to develop titles that you really get the most out of.

To send us general feedback, simply send an email to feedback@packtpub.com, and mention the book title via the subject of your message.

If there is a book that you need and would like to see us publish, please send us a note in the **SUGGEST A TITLE** form on www.packtpub.com or email suggest@packtpub.com.

If there is a topic that you have expertise in and you are interested in either writing or contributing to a book on, see our author guide on www.packtpub.com/authors.

Customer support

Now that you are the proud owner of a Packt book, we have a number of things to help you to get the most from your purchase.

Errata

Although we have taken every care to ensure the accuracy of our content, mistakes do happen. If you find a mistake in one of our books—maybe a mistake in the text or the code—we would be grateful if you would report this to us. By doing so, you can save other readers from frustration, and help us to improve subsequent versions of this book. If you find any errata, please report them by visiting http://www.packtpub.com/support, selecting your book, clicking on the **let us know** link, and entering the details of your errata. Once your errata are verified, your submission will be accepted and the errata added to any list of existing errata. Any existing errata can be viewed by selecting your title from http://www.packtpub.com/support.

Piracy

Piracy of copyright material on the Internet is an ongoing problem across all media. At Packt, we take the protection of our copyright and licenses very seriously. If you come across any illegal copies of our works, in any form, on the Internet, please provide us with the location address or web site name immediately so that we can pursue a remedy.

Please contact us at `copyright@packtpub.com` with a link to the suspected pirated material.

We appreciate your help in protecting our authors, and our ability to bring you valuable content.

Questions

You can contact us at `questions@packtpub.com` if you are having a problem with any aspect of the book, and we will do our best to address it.

1
What Can Mahara Do for Me?

So, you're interested in Mahara? Maybe you are already using it, but you are wondering if you are using it well. Maybe you've recently heard of Mahara and you are wondering if this is actually the ePortfolio solution you were looking for? Or, maybe you have been told you have to use it and you just need to get a sense of what Mahara is all about?

In subsequent chapters of this book, we will be digging into the nitty-gritty of getting your Mahara up and running and then making it practically work for you as a learner or as a Mahara Staff Member. This particular book is not specifically pitched at helping Mahara Site Administrators. Therefore, before we start getting down to the practical basics of Mahara, we need you to try to understand the big picture of what Mahara is about.

In this chapter, we will:

- ◆ Introduce you to the concept of ePortfolios
- ◆ Think about some of the different ways in which you can use Mahara
- ◆ Introduce you to the three fictional case studies used as examples in this book
- ◆ Learn why Mahara is the best option out there for your ePortfolio building and reflective learning
- ◆ Encourage you to become a member of the online Mahara community at `http://mahara.org`

So, let's get on with it!

Portfolios go electronic

You have been learning things since the day you were born. I have just gloried at my little four-year-old boy's first-ever picture of a cowboy on a horse (it's great!) and I will always remember the wooden toy truck I myself made in my woodwork class when I was a teenager. I also proudly remember the written design paper I had to write for my exams about how I actually made that wooden truck, but I have now lost that design paper, I have no idea where it has gone. Today, I am heavily involved with online distance learning, more specifically ePortfolios, and rarely a day goes when I don't learn something new.

Now, the thing is, all I have now are memories of my wooden truck, but, IF I had access back then to a digital ePortfolio, I could have kept a copy of that design paper. I could have scanned it into my computer and stored it as an image (if I hadn't created it digitally in the first place). I could have also stored a video of the sixteen year-old me showing off my wooden truck and I could have taken digital snapshots of the truck from all angles. If I was feeling really adventurous, I could have combined all these elements together and written about—or videoed myself speaking about—how I conceived the idea and how I actually made it.

Maybe my friends were really impressed with my wooden truck and wanted to know how to make it, so they could make one too. So, maybe I decided I was going to create a web page to show them. I could add all these videos, pictures, and commentaries to create a really useful and detailed resource page for my friends. Perhaps, I didn't (yet) want the world to know about my new carpentry skills—especially not Barry down the road from the rival school. In this case, I could have set up a special group so only the people I selected would be able to view my wooden truck page. Maybe one of my friends really liked the truck, and showed it to his Dad who was an engineer. Suppose they made one using my web page too, but with some tips from his Dad, they made one that went faster. He then started a forum discussing the improvements they had made. Then, perhaps another couple of my friends joined in and got really excited. They shared with the group their own modifications that they had researched on the Internet, uploaded a picture of an improved version to the group, and suggested we all got together once a week to work on one together and enter it in the county wooden truck championship.

And all along, without us being aware, let's imagine our teachers looking on smiling. They were watching us learn collaboratively and reflectively. They were watching us develop our IT skills and start off down the path of lifelong learning and collaborative working. They were watching us record our new-found learning and skills along with developing complex social networking skills. The teachers were all happy that this was taking place in a safe "walled garden" where only people to whom the school had given permission could access our work. The woodwork teacher sat back in his chair with a warm smile on his face. He knew he had taught me something of much greater worth than a wooden truck.

However, this is all pure fantasy. I did not have access to an ePortfolio that had all this functionality, and the Internet back then was not much more than a concept.

Towards an ePortfolio-enabled future

I am now, however, a fully ePortfolio-enabled-Dad and I am therefore, this afternoon, going to help my son (Salvador) to upload that picture of a cowboy on a horse. In future, he can share that picture with his friends, and possibly with some other junior artistic talents, online. He is about to embark upon a lifelong learning journey, and now he (with a little help from Dad), can keep a record of his learning into posterity.

I, myself, also see the need to store and share the knowledge I am gathering about my professional life online. I want to work in a community of professionals (like yourself) using ePortfolios, who I can buzz with, share ideas with, and grow with. I want to engage with a professional community who I can give to and learn from. I want to keep my personal reflections and files to myself sometimes, to share some with my colleagues, and some to share with the rest of the world. I wish to create pages as I see fit, not according to some pre-designed fixed template. I want to fully use my creative skills to design pages that I feel fit with my personal and professional style. I cannot do these things with Facebook or Beebo; I need the enhanced functionality and privacy that a socially interactive ePortfolio such as Mahara uses.

For both Salvador's needs and my own, I am going to use Mahara.

Ways of using Mahara

We've already started to look at how Mahara could be used for school children and professionally. However, this is just the tip of the iceberg. Mahara can be used in lots of different ways towards lots of different ends. Here are just a few different examples:

- A **Recruitment Agency** might use Mahara to forge links between job seekers and employers, employers with other employers, and job seekers with other job seekers.
- A **university or college** might use Mahara as a reflective learning platform for ALL of their students following ALL DIFFERENT TYPES of learning programs.
- A **student's union** might use Mahara as a vehicle for members of its clubs and societies to share their knowledge and their passions. For example, football, canoeing, the darts team, political groups, and so on.
- A **school teacher** might use Mahara to get her small group of students working together on a curriculum-related topic.
- A **professional body** may wish to set up Mahara for communicating with members and for the continuous professional development of its members.
- A **private training provider** might use Mahara as a way for learners to collate and submit their work for assessment as part of their qualification.
- A **group of friends** may wish to use Mahara to communicate and collaborate in a much more controlled way than Facebook or Beebo.

◆ A **group of professionals** from different organizations/locations may wish to work together on sharing best practice ideas and support each other through a variety of challenging situations. For example, a group of social workers.

◆ A **large organization** or corporation could use Mahara for their informal knowledge management processes, encouraging people in similar roles in different branches to work together in online communities of practice.

The list goes on...

In this book, we want you to look at the many ways you can use Mahara to fit your own specific situation. To help you do this, we will often be illustrating the different things you can do with Mahara by using any of these three imaginary case studies.

Case study one: Punam from Pennytown Primary

Punam, who is a teacher at Pennytown Primary, is taking her 9-year old students through a project on the Tudors. She is running on an institutional-themed Mahara that is set up on "Schools Online", a large, county-wide Mahara implementation for school teachers, who are working in a fictional English county called Rurishire.

Punam will be helping her students to work as a class group in order to gather files and discuss their learning. She doesn't just want them to upload a whole load of files, she wants them to organize files and data in a meaningful way, just like a paper-based project. This will mean she wants her students to create **views** in smaller working groups for their class project. She likes the idea of smaller working groups as this will allow her students to start working collaboratively. She likes the fact that Mahara facilitates this by allowing you both to set up different groups and to create a collaboratively created "group view".

What does View mean?

View is the Mahara word for a web page that we create ourselves in order to display our information. I like the word *View* for this because it tells me that I am creating a web page for people to look at (a nice view) AND it also suggests to me that I am expected to express my ideas and opinions (that is, my views) on this type of web page.

Some of her student's parents have come up to her and expressed concerns about online safety. One of their children has been the victim of cyber-bullying. She is quite happy that Mahara addresses this concern as, unlike Facebook, the only people that have access to the site are those that have been given permission by the school. The local education authority has set a policy that any adult who has access to this site must have passed a police check. If there are any concerns about other children, she can request that the administrator accesses all the views and forum posts so that she can find out who was responsible, and request suspension of the user if appropriate. She can happily reassure the parents that this is a walled garden site where their children are safe. There is even a facility for the learners themselves to **Report Objectionable Material** to the administrators should they stumble across any.

Case study two: Janet Norman from Pharmaceuticals International Inc. (PI Inc.)

Janet is a learning technologist who holds overarching responsibility for PI Inc.'s international corporate university. Each country, indeed, each and every branch that she represents has its own local learning agenda.

As a learning technologist, she wants to encourage informal, personalized, and reflective learning. She knows that spending time encouraging reflection and CPD (continuous professional development) helps to:

◆ Develop staff skills, creating a better workforce

◆ Increase staff morale

◆ Encourage the development of professionalism

◆ Increase staff retention as staff feel more valued

◆ Encourage innovation, which will help give PI Inc. an edge over their competitors

◆ Give out a strong corporate message about investment in people

However, Janet's main focus is implementing Mahara to facilitate informal, international knowledge transfer processes. She wants to spend some time setting up different types of **groups**. She can see the benefit of setting up groups to work on a variety of research projects being carried out throughout the organization. She is hopeful that the group members are going to make use of Mahara's blogging features to keep everyone up-to-date with their particular projects. There are currently three pilot studies being carried out in England, Peru, and Spain for a new cancer drug and she wants these three research groups to collaborate together and discuss early findings. She also wants to set up some international groups of practice and collaborate together in the hope that this will lead to some useful organizational innovations. She also wants to set up some groups, that select individuals can access from outside the company, to bring in some fresh ideas and perspectives, whilst also contributing to the wider pharmaceutical community.

What does Group mean?

This is Mahara's word for an online community that users can either:

◆ Join

◆ Request membership of

◆ Be invited to

◆ Or (sometimes) be selected into in a more controlled way

You can use groups in a variety of ways, but they are predominately used in Mahara to develop, stimulate, and support both social and learning activities in a social networking context.

PI Inc. are therefore running their own large international Mahara implementation with a range of their own institutions. Janet's people will be SHARING their knowledge. PI Inc. will be CAPTURING their knowledge before they leave. And, by engaging in this process, Janet's staff members will be CREATING new and innovative knowledge that PI Inc. can make use of as they expand into the future.

Case study three: Neil from Training 4 Work

Neil trains and assesses learners who are taking national vocational qualifications with a private training provider called Training 4 Work. He is helping 16-19 year olds to gain their vocational qualifications in electrical engineering. Although Training 4 Work only has about fifteen people in its staff, they have installed their own organizational Mahara because they like to have control over their own site.

Neil is also keen to use the resume-builder feature of Mahara. He has a number of links with local businesses for work placements, and he prides himself on the high percentage of learners that go on to full-time positions. He knows if he can get all his learners to input all their information into the resume builder and create an online resume, not only will this make matching his learners to work placements easier, this will also really impresses prospective employers.

Neil knows that, at the moment, his learners' files and evidence are stored all over the place in a variety of locations. Some of the homework is currently handed in as paper assignments. Some assessors have video and audio evidence stored in their camcorders or on their laptops, with hand-written notes. Some other parts of the work that his learners have done are stored on the Training 4 Work desktops up in the computer room. His e-mail inbox is always stuffed with e-mails from students sending him files with huge attachments to check. Newer students want to submit evidence in an ePortfolio as they did at Uppertown Secondary School. Finally, when he makes on-site visits he finds his students have often forgotten to bring their evidence with them, leading to yet another wasted trip! Assessing has become a complete nightmare! He spends more time actually trying to find the evidence than he does teaching and supporting his students.

Neil says he will make extensive use of Mahara's **artefacts** feature. This will allow him to get the students to organize their "digital stuff" (or artefacts) into one central location where they can then share them with him, verifiers, and also other students easily, using views. As it will be accessible anywhere anytime there is Internet access, students now can't forget or lose their work. He has also been set up as a Mahara Staff Member (more on this in Chapter 7), which will allow him to force his learners into a Controlled Group—into which the learners will submit views evidencing their learning, which can then be formally assessed. Neil will, of course, set up a template view for learners to copy and build their evidence upon. The learners will not be able to edit their submitted views again until Neil releases them with his feedback. Neil needs this sort of control because his accrediting body and external verifiers require him to have it.

What does Artefact mean?

Artefact is the Mahara word for a bit of digital "stuff"—such as files, blogs, and profile or resume information. We control other people's access to our stuff by deciding for ourselves who can see the artefacts we choose to display in our own views.

Neil can't wait to start using Mahara! It will make his life so much easier. He can give online coaching as and when needed, there will be no more forgotten files and wasted trips, and most importantly his students will learn more—and learn to reflect more, as this will help them not only to gain their all-important qualifications but also to become more valuable employees.

Time for action – looking at some real-life Maharas

1. In your browser, go to `http://mahara.org`. Right there on the front page are some examples of Mahara in action. This page itself is also a Mahara!

2. Click on one of the views in the middle of the page. There are lots of different ones to choose from. Click around and have a look at the variety of practical uses you can use Mahara for! Can you see a view in there created by one of the authors of this book?

A teachers' forum - Mark Osbome, Albany Senior High

3. Visit `http://mahara.tdm.info` to have a look at our website We are using Mahara as a member's only subsection of our company's public-facing website. Feel free to register yourself as a user (right-hand column). You might find some interesting views on ePortfolios and e-Learning and e-Business in general in here.

4. Visit `http://demo.mahara.org` to go to Mahara's demo site. This is Mahara's demo site. Yet another Mahara site! This is a really useful site as you can register and have a bit of a play around with Mahara safely in here.

What just happened?

You have just started to look at Mahara and what it can do.

- ◆ You've had a look at some examples of Mahara in practice.
- ◆ You've looked at the demo site where you can have a play around with Mahara before installing it.

Why Mahara?

While they are not as old as the three-ring-binder and the artist's portfolio folder, digital ePortfolios have, nevertheless, actually been around for a long, long time. Have you ever stored your learning data on floppy disks, USB sticks, CDs, or DVDs? Maybe you've even created your own, personal Dreamweaver-produced or HTML/CSS website, or used a blogging engine such as WordPress, or Content Management Systems such as Drupal or Joomla, or maybe you have used a Course Management System such as Moodle to store your personal stuff. If you have, these are all types of ePortfolios, really.

None of these, however, were ever conceived to act as ePortfolio platforms in their own right. Mahara now gives us an ePortfolio system that is thoughtfully and specifically designed for the job in hand. It gives us our own "personalized learning environment". Mahara seeks to go beyond a basic ePortfolio and gives us a variety of other useful features to help us both to learn reflectively and to work collaboratively.

Mahara is therefore a platform for **personalized**, **reflective**, and **collaborative** learning:

Personalized learning

Twenty-first century learning no longer needs to be delivered on somebody else's agenda in a jug-and-mug delivery style. Mahara concerns itself with the personalization of the learning process.

- **Personalized Self-Presentation**: Mahara offers an easy-to-use web interface that allows you to design your own web pages (views), thereby, you will be organizing and presenting your own learning data in precisely the way you would like to present it.

- **Privacy**: If you want some place to collect your thoughts and files, you probably want these to remain private until you decide that you are ready to show them to someone else. In Mahara, you now have a pretty private* area on the Internet where you can keep your stuff such as files (documents, videos, audio clips, images, and so on). You can also use this private space to keep up your blog (another word for personal diary) and also your ever-changing profile and resume information.

 *only you and the system administrator(s) can access your files.

- **Accessible**: We can access our private stuff **whenever** we like from **wherever** we can log onto the Internet. Wow! This beats carrying our data around on a USB stick, doesn't it? No more forgotten or lost files. Access your files at work, at school, at the library, or even when you are sitting on the beach in Barbados. Mahara is giving you FREEDOM.

- **Transfer your data**: What about when you move schools and change companies? What happens to your data then? Many ePortfolios "lock you in" and you won't be able to transfer your data. Who wants that?

◆ **Access control**: In Mahara we, ourselves, retain the right to control who gets access over our own artefacts (those bits of digital stuff). We do this by setting up views (Mahara web pages) of our digital data artefacts and then deciding who gets to see them. It allows you to create groups so you can allow different people and groups to access different views. Well, you wouldn't want your boss seeing THAT picture of the office party would you? (This is another reason why Mahara is better than so many of those Web 2.0 social networking sites.) You might want to work with your suppliers on a joint marketing campaign, but do you REALLY want to share your company's sensitive financial reports with them, too? Mahara lets you satisfy all of these different needs neatly and easily.

Reflective learning

But Mahara offers more than just being a way to store and to show off your stuff to others. Mahara encourages you to "grow" as a learner by reflecting on your own learning journey.

◆ **Developing your own goals and skills**: Mahara encourages you to record, reflect on, and update your personal, academic, and work/career-related goals and skills. It has even created special sections just to facilitate this. Life is a journey, our dreams and objectives are in constant flux. If you've misplaced that notebook or scrap of paper with *New Year Resolutions* on it, how can you know if you've kept them? Now, with Mahara, you can easily check back to see that you are still on the right learning pathway. Everything is all in one place!

◆ **Keeping blogs**: Ever kept a diary or a journal? Ever made notes to yourself? Keeping a blog can be a very useful way to get someone to stop and think, to reflect on and to learn from their experiences or from the information they have had to study and process. Taking some time out to reflect and compose thoughts is a highly useful exercise. You can now keep as many blogs as you like, all in one place, stored together with your goals, skills, and files. You keep the blogs for yourself, not necessarily to publish them to others. You can, of course, move on to put your blogs into views for others to access if you want to, or if you are asked to! You can keep a personal blog, a work blog, a project blog, and a blog to share with your friends!

◆ **Integration with other platforms (including Web 2.0)**: Yes, Mahara is set up to allow for integrations with other online spaces. At the moment, you can call in RSS feeds from your blog (outside Mahara) or CMS. HTML filters are set up for Twitter, SlideShare, Skype, and so on. You can also very easily call in external videos from YouTube, TeacherTube, Google Video, and SciVee.tv and plans are afoot for more and more Web 2.0 integrations! Mahara can be seen as a personalized, reflective learning space where you can gather together all of your learning artefacts, storing them internally within Mahara or externally within other locations on the World Wide Web.

Collaborative learning

While Mahara is a self-oriented learning platform (many call it a Personalized Learning Environment or "PLE"), it also facilitates informal learning activity amongst friends and groups.

- **Making friends**: Many of us learn best when we are working together and reflecting openly with other people and so Mahara encourages community relationships. You can present your views with a different profile icon to different people and communities (see Chapter 5 for more details). You can message people from the contact details they display within Mahara, you can form a network of people with similar interests to yourself and add their views to a watchlist—which will let you know when they have updated their views. You can place feedback on other people's views and allow others to place feedback on yours in order that you can teach and learn from one another (see Chapter 5 for more details). Your online learning community is born!

- **Working and learning in groups**: Life is more fun when shared with others! It's time to get down to some LEARNING and WORKING together in groups! You can join and set up for yourself different types of groups for different types of learning communities (see Chapter 6 for more details). In your groups, you can share common files, you can share your own views for others to see, or work TOGETHER on views you create as a group. You can also engage in group discussion forums to really get your reflective learning into gear!

- **Course Groups**: Mahara staff members can set up Course Groups. These are special group types that enable learners to submit their views (web pages) to you for your formal "Assessment". This is an excellent way of tracking learners' progress on formal, evidence-based qualifications. We will talk more about this in Chapter 7 of this book.

- **Integration with Moodle**: Sometimes, it is useful for a teacher to take learners through a staged sequence of learning objectives using quizzes and other formal learning activities, performance on which can be assessed and reported on in a gradebook. Mahara deliberately doesn't provide that functionality. Mahara, is a place for informal learning. Mahara is NOT a Course Management System. Luckily, Mahara's "sister" program steps in here: Moodle (`http://moodle.org`). Moodle is a Course Management System that can be set up to run in the background of Mahara sharing SINGLE SIGN-ON access. This means Mahara users can set up and follow links within Mahara from which they can seamlessly migrate directly over to a formally taught and graded course that is running in a Moodle platform. (See *Moodle Administration*, also from Packt Publishing.) In future, we are going to be able to easily bring back the data we used in our Moodle course to our portfolio platform, and thereby, let our informal, ongoing, never-ending reflective learning experience resume once our taught course is done and dusted. Viva Mahara!

Pop quiz – what is important to you in an ePortfolio?

What do you need from an ePortfolio? Grade the ePortfolio criteria below with a number on a scale of 1-5, that is:

5= VITALLY IMPORTANT

4= REALLY IMPORTANT

3= IMPORTANT

2= NOT VERY IMPORTANT

1= NOT IMPORTANT AT ALL

The criteria (in no particular order):

- _____ The user OWNS their own data and can control who gets ACCESS to it.
- _____ The user gets their own FILE STORAGE area (like you get on your own computer, for example, My Documents), which they can access, modify, and control via the Internet.
- _____ The user's ePortfolio is PORTABLE, allowing them to migrate their data from provider to provider during their LIFELONG LEARNING journey.
- _____ The user gets opportunities for REFLECTIVE LEARNING via blogs, learning/career goal-setting, group projects, and so on.
- _____ The ePortfolio user gets opportunities for SOCIAL NETWORKING in interest groups with forum discussions.
- _____ The user gets creative freedom over the PERSONALIZED SELF-PRESENTATION of their own learning. They can stylize their "web pages" according to their own preferences/needs.
- _____ The user gets the chance to SHOW OFF their stuff to other people, for example, they can show their learning achievements and resume details, and so on to potential employers.
- _____ The ePortfolio allows a user to link in their stuff from Web 2.0 social sites such as YouTube, Twitter, or Facebook.
- _____ The user's personal ePortfolio INTEGRATES seamlessly with the learning programs they pursue on their Moodle Virtual Learning Environment (http://moodle.org).

- ◆ _____ Allowing the user their right to know that nothing untoward is happening to their data by OPENING the software SOURCE CODE to public view and scrutiny.

- ◆ _____ Allowing the learning provider organization their right to AVOID LOCKING IN their own AND their learners' personal data into a PROPRIETARY data format that belongs to a particular Software Company.

- ◆ _____ Using a community-supported OPEN SOURCE ePortfolio platform that is MODULAR and OPEN to MODIFICATION, meaning that providers can work collaboratively to make the platform work better for their common (and also for their very particular) ePortfolio needs.

- ◆ _____ The ePortfolio can be configured to offer controlled groups with a "SUBMIT for ASSESSMENT" process—allowing an assessor (or external verifier) to easily verify that a learner has done their work—in the same way that they would do with a paper-based or USB-stick-based portfolio assessment process.

- ◆ _____ While using the ePortfolio for formal assessment via accrediting bodies, the ePortfolio can be integrated with sophisticated open source ILP (Individual Learning Plan) and Assessment Manager Tools (such as The ULCC Personalization of Learning Framework: http://moodle.ulcc.ac.uk/course/view.php?id=139).

As you have probably already guessed, Mahara is capable of satisfying ALL of the above criteria.

Join the Mahara community

There is already a pretty vibrant and active international Mahara community working together over at http://mahara.org. Mahara is all about collaborative learning and it's a great idea for you to come and join in. Not only is it exciting to become part of this active community, but you can receive help and support, and as you become more confident, even start giving your own suggestions to the Mahara team and complete the circle, fully engaging in the collaborative spirit!

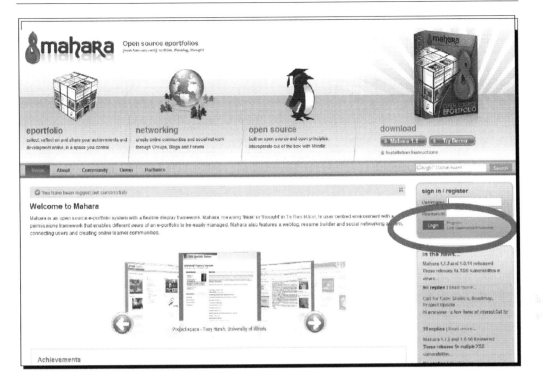

Have you ever seen a Maharan?

Some members of the Mahara community are starting to call themselves Maharans.

Time for action – registering and exploring further

1. **Go and register**: The very first thing that anyone will do on your Mahara site is log in. Head on over to `http://mahara.org` and click the option to **Register**, a small link, which you will find in the pale blue **Login** button in the top right-hand part of the screen. Once you've registered you can log in.

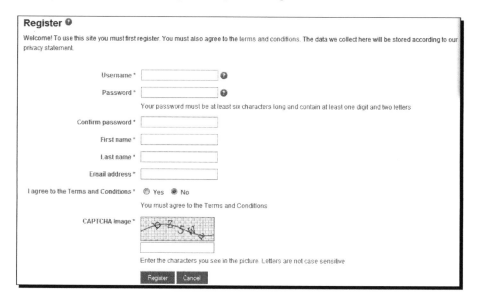

2. **Respond to your e-mail**: You will need to confirm your registration by clicking the link that has been sent to your e-mail address. Once you have done this, you will find yourself at `http://mahara.org`, which is itself a Mahara site.

3. **Let's find some people!:** Click on the **Community** tab, and then on the **Members** tab. Now let's see if you can find the authors! Can you see the **Query** box? Type in my name **Derrin** and see if you can find me?

4. **Let's look at some views**: Now you've found me, click on my name and why not click on one of my views? Here's another example of Mahara in action.

5. **Join a forum**: Click on the **Community** tab again, and now on the **Forums** tab. Can you see the **Support** forum? Its description is **Need help using or installing Mahara? Ask your questions here**. That's going to be useful to you, I bet! Why not subscribe to this forum by clicking on the **Subscribe** button. You will now be e-mailed with all the updates to this forum. Maybe there are other forums you might want to subscribe to. If you just want to browse a forum, just click on the name of the forum and you will be taken to a list of the posts.

6. **Have a look at the Mahara partners**: Click on the **Partners** tab. Mahara partners can help you with hosting, theming, training, coding, tweaking, extending, bug-fixing, problem-resolving, implementation consultancies, and, well, just about anything to do with Mahara, if you ask them nicely enough. All Mahara partners are excellent support agencies and, if you ARE really keen on using Mahara, you really should give one of the partners a shout.

What just happened?

You have just become a Maharan! Does it feel strange? You have:

◆ Registered on `http://mahara.org`

◆ Found Derrin and his Mahara views on `mahara.org`

◆ Joined the support forum

◆ Learned how to find a Mahara partner

Pop quiz – learning about http://mahara.org

These questions test what you have learned about `mahara.org`:

1. Why would you bother to register on `mahara.org`?
2. How would you find another `mahara.org` member?
3. Why would you join a forum?
4. How would you find a Mahara partner?

Have a go hero – pressing the buttons till it hurts

Some of us are *inchworms* who like information to be presented to us logically and sequentially. *Inchworms* like to be taken through a new process step-by-step. Others amongst us are *grasshoppers* who like to hop around bits of information wherever we find them and then gradually start piecing together the big picture of our understanding.

Inchworms are no better or worse than *grasshoppers*. We are just different.

This book is structured for *inchworms*, but we know you *grasshoppers* will easily be able to hop around our book and pick up on the useful bits.

Right now, though, be you an *inchworm* or a *grasshopper*, we want you to behave in a *grasshoppery* sort-of-a-way as you engage in this task (take a deep breath, *inchworms*, you may just enjoy it!).

Go to `http://demo.mahara.org` and register yourself:

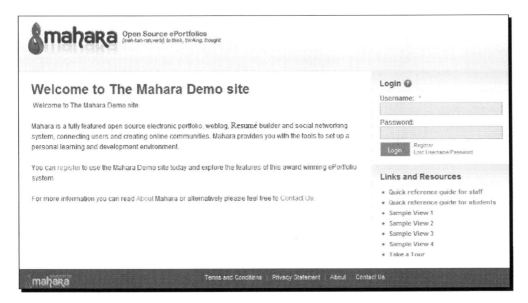

This is a test-bed site where you should feel free to go around and bang all of the buttons until it hurts. You really can't do any damage in there so just go in and explore and experiment. Click the links and buttons and follow wherever your mouse leads you. This will stand you in very good stead for when we walk you through Mahara's functionalities later on in this book.

You may also find it useful to have a look at some of the links and resources you will find in the right-hand column. If you click **Take a Tour**, you will see a nice introductory video for Mahara that Andy Kirk has uploaded onto SciVee.tv. There are also some nice example views here (you will be creating your own views later) as well as a couple of really useful Quick reference guides: one for Mahara staff and another for Mahara students.

Lookin' good...

One of the beauties of Mahara is that it is easy for a web designer to make some pretty significant changes to the theme. Notice that the `http://mahara.org` site looks really quite different from the default Mahara site that we will be working on throughout the rest of this book.

Summary

We learned a lot in this chapter about why Mahara ePortfolios are useful and what will be involved in making a Mahara site work.

Specifically, we understood what an ePortfolio essentially is and looked at possible uses of Mahara. We also looked at some real-life Mahara sites and learned what is so special about the Mahara ePortfolio. Hopefully, you became a member of the Mahara community by joining at `http://mahara.org`. If you did, you'd have browsed around `mahara.org` and looked at some of the useful features. Finally, some of you will have gotten an initial feel for Mahara by clicking around in the demo area `http://demo.mahara.org` and also in `http://mahara.org` itself.

In this chapter, we also discussed the importance of personalized, reflective, and collaborative learning.

Now that we've learned about the big picture as to why Mahara matters, you're probably keen to start working in your live Mahara environment? First of all, you will need to start practically entering data, uploading and setting up some stuff that you can use in the system—which is the topic of the next chapter.

2
Getting Started with Mahara

Now that we have understood some of the potential of Mahara it's time to get started. The very first thing you are going to do is to register for a Mahara site, log in, and set up your own personal profile page.

In this chapter we shall:

- ◆ Register to join the demonstration Mahara that accompanies this book
- ◆ Explore the Mahara user interface
- ◆ Enter your personal information
- ◆ Think about what goes into our own profile page and start configuring it
- ◆ Have a brief introduction to the Mahara text editor

By the end of the chapter, you will have set up your own profile page in Mahara and be ready to start adding your "stuff".

Registering with a Mahara site

I'm sure you can't wait to get inside a Mahara site and have a look around. Luckily, for this book we have created a demonstration site, so you can do just that.

Usually, a Mahara site administrator will provide you with your own username and password so that you can log in straight away. Sometimes though, to join a Mahara site, you will have to register.

Let's have a look at some of the Mahara sites available on the Internet that you can register to join:

◆ http://maharaforbeginners.tdm.info: This is the demonstration site for this book. Register here to work through the examples in each chapter.

◆ http://demo.mahara.org: This is the default Mahara installation that is kept up-to-date. This site is used by newcomers who want to get to know the features of Mahara for the first time.

◆ http://mahara.org: This is Mahara's own website which is a highly stylized version of a Mahara site. You can register here to follow and take part in discussions about all things related to Mahara.

If you have login details for your own Mahara site, you might want to skip the following *Time for action* section and get straight into logging in. However, we recommend that you register to join the demonstration site accompanying this book. Along with going through the examples in this book, the demo site will also have some forums, groups, and Views too.

So, let's practice registering for a Mahara site. You may have already registered and explored the Mahara.org website in chapter one, here we will look again at how to register to join a Mahara website but in bit more detail.

Time for action – registering onto the demonstration site

1. Enter http://maharaforbeginners.tdm.info into your browser's address bar.

2. Click the **Register** link found at the bottom of the **Login** block:

3. Fill in the registration form; enter a **Username** and **Password**.

4. Hang on! Before clicking the button to register, you really should read the **Terms and Conditions** and privacy statement before you agree to them.

5. Then click the **Register** button at the bottom of the page. Hopefully, you will now get an on-screen message telling you that you have successfully registered! If not, don't worry, you will get a message on the screen letting you know what went wrong; correct the problem and try again.

6. Now that your details have been accepted, you will receive an e-mail from the Mahara site. In the e-mail, click the link provided to register.

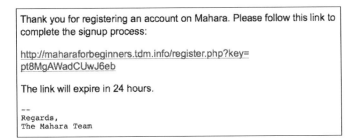

7. A new window will open in your browser showing that you have logged into the Mahara site:

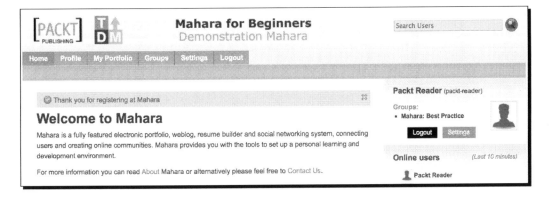

What just happened?

You have just registered yourself onto the Mahara demo site for this book by entering some valid details and responding to an automated e-mail.

When registering for some Mahara sites, you might find that there is an extra drop-down option inviting you to select an institution. You can read about institutions in Chapter 7.

Logging in for the first time

If you have just registered for the demo site, then you will already be logged into Mahara. In the future though, you will need to know how to log in for yourself. By now you should have a username and password, either for the demonstration site or provided by your Mahara administrator in your own Mahara. We're going to be using those details to log in.

Time for action – logging in

1. Once your account has been registered, you log in to the site whenever you visit by using the **Login** block on the home page. Type your **Username** and **Password** in and click **Login**.

2. If this is the first time you are logging in, it is likely that you will be asked to change your password. If this is the case, enter your **New Password** twice and click **Change password**.

3. That's all there is to it! You have just logged into Mahara for the first time.

What just happened?

You have just learned how to log into Mahara for the first time.

Logging in is easy, if you can remember your login details. If you have forgotten your details, then don't worry; Mahara provides a useful way of retrieving your username and password, all you need is your e-mail address (let's hope you don't forget that!).

To retrieve your details, just click on the **Lost Username/Password** link at the bottom of the **Login** box. You will then see this page:

Forgotten your username or password? ❷

If you have forgotten your username or password, enter the email address listed in your profile and we will send you a message you can use to give yourself a new password.

If you know your username and have forgotten your password, you can also enter your username instead.

Email address or username *   packreader@email.com

Send request

Enter you e-mail address and click **Send request**. You will find your login details in an e-mail at the address you just entered.

Use two different browsers to log in more than one user on the same computer.
You may face problems in Mahara if you try to log into the same site more than once with the same browser on the same computer. The best thing to do is to use two different internet browsers if you want two users to be logged in at the same time (for example, Firefox and Safari).

I'm sure at this point you can't wait to start pressing a few buttons to try out Mahara's functionality. But first, we need to have a look at some of the important features of Mahara's layout, which is the topic of the next section.

Mahara's user interface—finding your way around

One of the beauties of Mahara is that the menu options are laid out very simply. After clicking through the menu options a few times, you will find that you instinctively know where the option you are looking for is located.

A word on Mahara themes

Before we look in more detail at navigation, it is important to realize that Mahara can be themed. This means you are able to change the visual layout of Mahara—the header section can be configured to have a different logo, layout can be altered, and font size/color can be adjusted (among other things). Theming doesn't affect Mahara content, but only the way it looks.

The demonstration site theme we are using in this book is an adaptation of "Default", which is the theme you begin with. The only difference is that we have made the theme orange and black whereas the default is green. Don't worry if your Mahara has a slightly different coloring or layout, all the "content" should be the same. Now, we move on to menus.

In Mahara there are two types of menus; the main menu and submenus. Let's take a look.

The main menu and submenus

The main menu is the most important feature for navigating around your Mahara. This is because it appears on almost every page that you visit and contains options for linking to all the important sections of your portfolio. You can see it at the top of your Mahara page and it will look a bit like this:

We will be looking in detail at each of the sections of the main menu as we go through this book. Let's get a quick idea of where each button takes us:

- **Home**: Clicking here returns you to the Mahara homepage.
- **Profile**: Click here to navigate to your personal profile space. Click into this area to put in your own personal details and to set up your own profile page.
- **My Portfolio**: Clicking here takes you to your portfolio. In this area you can add your own "stuff" and start creating some web pages.
- **Groups**: Click here to take you to social aspects of Mahara. You can join groups, access forums, and get in contact with other Mahara users in this section.
- **Settings**: Here you can control the finer details of your Mahara.
- **Logout**: This logs you out of your Mahara.

Each of the menu items discussed above, with the exception of **Home** and **Logout**, has its own menu associated with it. These are what we call submenus. Submenus are found below the main menu. Here, is the submenu for the **Profile** section:

Site blocks

Site blocks are another important navigational tool. In a standard theme, they appear on the right-hand side of the screen. Site blocks contain quick links to sections of your portfolio, removing the need to navigate through the main menu and submenus. This is the case for the main site block that you use to log out of Mahara, access site settings, and link to your personal profile (by clicking the picture):

There are site blocks that also display useful information such as the online users' block that shows the users of the site who have been online within a certain time period. By default, this is the **Last 10 minutes**:

The footer

The footer is located at the bottom of your Mahara page and contains links to **Terms and Conditions**, **Privacy Statement**, **About** page (that tells you a bit about Mahara), and a **Contact Us** page (that allows you to get in contact with the site administrator). Mahara provides templates for some of these pages, but your site administrator should have adapted them to your own organizational requirements. There will also be an image linking to Mahara.org. Here is what the footer should look like:

Setting up your own profile

For the remainder of this chapter, we are going to concentrate on the **Profile** tab of the main menu. The very first thing that most Mahara users want to do is customize their own profile space, making it unique to them. We will show you how to do that. For the following examples, we will be working with Janet Norman of PI Inc, showing you how she has configured her profile space. Why not set up your own profile in the demonstration site as you work through the examples? Let's start by looking at profile information.

Profile information

Later you will set up your own profile page—showing yourself and your knowledge off to others in an attractively personalized way. However, before you do that, you need to add some profile information. Your profile information is the first example we will see of "stuff" that you can add to Mahara. When we say **stuff** we simply mean information, or items that can then be viewed later or arranged into web pages, which we will see when we look at your profile page.

You are now going to set up some profile information as "stuff" that you can select from and use. We will look at three types of profile information—your profile itself, profile icons, along with your resumé, goals, and skills.

Editing your profile

Let's show you how to edit your profile. Any information you enter into your profile is private from everyone except the Mahara Site Administrators. You will get to choose who can view what, later on in the Mahara process.

Time for action – editing your profile

1. Click the **Profile** button on the main menu.

2. You will notice that Mahara has opened the Profile submenu. The **Edit Profile** tab is selected when you first enter your profile space. Let's take a quick look at Janet's profile. You will notice that the **About Me** tab is selected. Janet has already entered her name.

3. Say something about yourself! Scroll down to the **Introduction** section of the **About Me** page and enter some text. Here is what Janet Norman typed in:

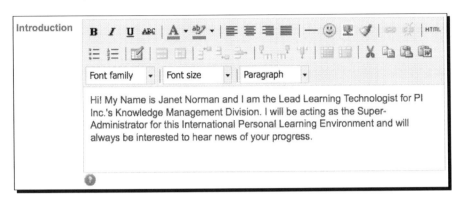

4. Whenever you make any changes, click the **Save Profile** button at the bottom of the page.

5. Next, click the **Contact Information** to the right of the **About me** tab.

6. You will see that you are expected to fill out some telephone numbers and addresses. The first thing you should notice is that you can have more than one e-mail address in a Mahara site. To add another e-mail address, click the link to **Add email address**. The e-mail address will receive a confirmation e-mail from the Mahara site and you will have to go to your e-mail account and follow the link to confirm it is genuine.

7. You can now use radio buttons to toggle which e-mail address you would like to use as default for your account. This selection is important because it is at this address that you will receive system messages. You will also notice that you can delete an e-mail address by clicking the small, red-colored cross to the right of the e-mail address.

8. Fill in your contact information on this page. Remember, you don't have to complete all the fields if you don't want to.

9. Click the tab called **Messaging**. Mahara will bring together the types of people you are likely to engage with in live text, audio, and video conferences. People can display these contact details to each other in their profile page and other web pages. Enter your contact details for the facilities you use on this page. If you are still not using live conferencing tools, perhaps now is the time to start thinking about it.

10. Finally, click the tab called **General**. On this page enter your **Occupation** and **Industry** (remember to click the **Save Profile** button when you have finished). Janet Norman typed this:

What just happened?

You have just completed your profile by entering some information about yourself, including your personal information, what messaging/conference tools you use, and your Industry background.

Both the **Contact Information** and **Messaging** information are **private** and will only be seen **if** you add them to a web page. This is because you don't necessarily want anybody in the Mahara site to be able to see your telephone number and address for security reasons.

Help!

If you have found so far that you wish you had a bit more information about what certain options do, then don't worry! Mahara is very well documented software. On most pages, you will see little question mark icons, that look something like this: ⊙ . If ever in doubt, click on these and you will be given very useful and specific help relating to your area of doubt.

Let's now continue to add some more stuff into our profile, with profile icons.

Profile icons

Profile icons bring your profile to life! They are the first thing that people see about you when they are interacting with you in different areas of the site.

Mahara allows you to upload up to five different profile icons. This becomes very useful (as we will see in Chapter 4) when you are making web pages out of your stuff. You can present yourself to different audiences in different ways, simply by altering your profile icon. For example, you can display a serious passport photo to your professional work colleagues, a more informal photo to your closest work colleagues, perhaps an avatar for public groups where you would like to be a bit more anonymous, and a picture of you having fun at a party for some of your more social interactions.

Time for action – uploading your profile icons

Let's get a few different profile icons online.

1. Click the Profile submenu button called **Profile Icons**.

2. Click **Browse** to find the profile icon you want to upload from your computer or USB stick (or wherever).

3. Don't forget to add an **Image Title** for your profile icon before you click the upload button.

4. You are allowed to upload up to five profile icons and you can delete any icon at any point. You will need to choose one of your icons as your default profile icon which should probably be a fairly sensible one. Janet Norman has already uploaded two profile icons:

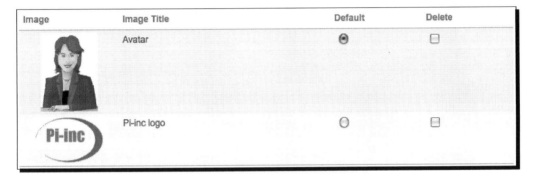

Image	Image Title	Default	Delete
	Avatar	◉	☐
	Pi-inc logo	○	☐

What just happened?

You have just uploaded a profile icon to represent yourself in your Mahara site. As we saw in the *Time for action* section, Janet has uploaded two icons. One of these is an avatar of herself and the other is the company logo. She plans to use the company logo in places where she would like to appear more professional, whereas the avatar will be used more generally.

Make yourself an avatar!

An avatar is simply a character or cartoon representation of yourself. If you don't want a passport photograph as your profile icon, an avatar is a good alternative. There are many websites that help you create your own. A few of the most fun include the Simpsons Avatar Maker (http://www.simpsonsmovie.com), DoppelMe (http://www.doppelme.com), and Mr Picassohead (http://www.mrpicassohead.com).

Editing your resumé goals and skills

No longer will you need to trawl through ancient hard drives trying to find the resumé you last wrote five years ago. Instead, you can keep your resumé information within your Mahara system and update it when you make changes. How impressive will you look when you show your resumé to your prospective employer as a web page rather than on a piece of paper.

There are three tabs remaining in the profile submenu that allow us to add stuff to our site. The remaining things we can add are:

◆ Resumé information: You can record your career and educational achievements.

◆ Goals information: Here you can set ourselves personal, academic, and career-related targets for your future.

◆ Skills information: You can record for yourselves what you perceive to be your personal, academic, and work-related skills.

----- Punam from Pennytown Primary thinks -----

It might be too early to get my children writing up their resumé, but goals and skills will certainly be a useful process for me. I would like to enter my goals and skills now and look back at them again in a few months' time to check that I am achieving the goals I set for myself and that I am continuously expanding upon and consolidating my skills.

----- Janet Norman form PI-Inc thinks -----

PI-Inc needs our staff to get into the habit of adding their resumé information within our system. Before Mahara we never had such a neat way of keeping resumés together.

----- **Neil from Training 4 Work thinks** -----

I didn't like the word "Resumé" so I looked through the Mahara forums and found out how to change it to "CV". Some of the learners we take on at "Training 4 Work" already have work, but others are looking for jobs. I will be able to get learners to compile their CV, goals, and skills information into web pages that can be linked to. The link can then be e-mailed to their potential employers. I will also get my learners to show video clips of themselves doing engineering work and to put up audio clips of me talking about how they have progressed during their time with us. They might even post up a blog on their job search progress; there are many possibilities.

Time for action – editing your resumé goals and skills

1. Click the **My Resumé** tab on the **Profile** submenu.

2. The first two text-entry boxes ask you to type in a cover letter and also some information about your interests. Type in some information here to get you started. Don't forget to click the **Save** button immediately after you have entered your information.

3. Now scroll down to see the contact information that has been carried across from the **Contact Information** page you edited earlier.

4. As you work your way down the page, you will be prompted to fill in your personal information, employment history, education history, and so on. Fill in the sections that are relevant to you.

5. Click into the **My Goals** tab and write your three different types of goals.

6. Click into the **My Skills** tab and write your three different types of skills.

What just happened?

You just edited your resumé, your goals and your skills. This information is now stored in Mahara. The beauty of this of course is that you need to go through this process only once, then in the future you will only need to make updates depending on changes in career or skill sets. This is much better than having to update a word processed document!

You should regularly pop back and update your profile information. Also, you should think about using different e-mail accounts within Mahara for different purposes and audiences. Mahara encourages you to do this so that you can receive similar sorts of messages from similar groups of people in separate places.

Mahara asks you to set up a **Blog Address** as part of your contact information. Perhaps you could use Mahara itself to create a web page that collates your public-facing blogs. You could then enter this page as your blog in your contact information.

Most of all, we encourage you to use Mahara to become a reflective learner. It is not only a useful self-developmental process to use blogs to articulate, capture, and refine your everyday thinking processes, it can also be a useful self-developmental process to:

- **Set yourself concrete academic, educational, and career-related goals that you then strive to achieve**:

   It is all too easy to just roll on from one year to the next. Mahara is encouraging us to be a bit more proactive with our lives than this. Why not push yourself? Set yourself some forward-looking targets and then strive to achieve them.

- **Honestly, openly, and critically self-evaluate your skills**:

   It is as important that you are able to identify what you *can* do as it is for you to be able to identify what you want to be able to do or achieve. Use the Mahara Skills section to see if you can be honest and open with yourself about where your own skills and strengths actually lie. Are you intellectually and emotionally mature enough to actually be able to identify what you are good at? Many people aren't. Using Mahara can help you to get better at doing this.

Pop quiz – understanding your profile information

- How many profile icons can you upload to your profile?
- In which section of your portfolio should you be adding career related targets?
   - Goals
   - Skills
   - Contact Information
   - My Resumé

Have a go hero – doing more with your profile information

You saw in the last section that you can add links to your messaging addresses in your profile information. Mahara is encouraging you to play with some live messenger and audio/video conferencing clients such as Skype and Jabber. If you are not using these already, visit www.skype.com or www.jabber.org and sign up. You can also add your MSN, AIM, or YAHOO! accounts. You can now share this information with other users on your profile page as we'll see in the next section, so people have a different way of getting in touch with you.

Your profile page

Now for the exciting bit, your profile page. Before we start, let's introduce a bit more Mahara terminology. Throughout this chapter we have been hinting that all the 'stuff' you have been uploading as profile information can be added to your own web pages. Mahara still uses a special name for these web pages—Views. Be prepared though, in the near future, this name seems set to change to something like web page or just page.

One of the most important Views you create in Mahara will be your profile page. Whichever of your other Views other people look at, they are likely at some point want to come back to your profile page to find out exactly who it is writing and recording all the fascinating stuff they are reading, listening to, and watching. All they have to do is to click your name or your profile icon wherever they see it and they will be taken straight to your profile page. Let's get our first look at your profile page.

Time for action – viewing and investigating your profile page

1. View your profile page by clicking on the **View Profile Page** tab.

2. You will find this under the **Profile** button on the main menu. If you entered information into the **About Me** page, you will notice this is showing in your profile.

3. Scroll down the page and look at the different sections. You probably won't see many more sections filled in as you're only just starting. Can you see the sections for **My Views**. This is probably empty at the moment but as you start adding Views, they will appear here.

4. Janet Norman from PI–Inc's profile page looks like this so far:

About Me

Hi! My name is Janet Norman and I am the Lead Learning Technologist for PI inc.'s Knowledge Management Division. I will be acting as the Super-Administrator for this international Personal Learning Environment and will always be interested to hear news of your progress.

My Friends

Try searching for new friends to grow your network!

Wall

Maximum 1500 characters per post. You can format your post using BBCode. Learn more

Make your post private? ☐
Post

No wall posts to display

5. Have a look at your **Wall**. Try typing a message directly into the box in the **Wall** section and click on the **Post** button. If you are just playing around with it at the moment, it might be best to check the little box **Make your post private**, so no one else can see it.

6. Go and have a look at Derrin's Mahara.org profile page at `http://mahara.org/user/view.php?id=106` This will allow you to see what a more populated profile page can look like (you won't need to sign in because Derrin's Mahara View is toggled to "Allow public access"):

What just happened?

You just viewed your profile page for the first time ever and learned a bit about how it is initially organized. Let's look at a few of the new things we just encountered.

When you add your personal information, Mahara remembers it all and uses it to automatically enter details to save you time. Information from your profile is autoloaded into different sections of your profile page

At the moment, your profile page will be looking quite empty. You probably noticed that there were sections in there for groups, friends, and Views, but no information shown. This is because we haven't even added any groups, friends, or Views yet!

The profile page wall

We just found out how to post on the wall on our profile page, but what is the profile page wall and what is it used for?

The wall gets used as a place where people post messages that are directly and publicly aimed at you (as opposed to messages in forums that are aimed at closed groups of people and system messages that are privately sent to you). Anybody who visits your profile page will see what has been written to you on your wall. This means you have to think carefully before writing on someone else's wall, as it is open to the world.

We also touched on the idea of making your own post private. This essentially turns your wall post into a message as it can't be seen by everyone. A private wall post will be viewable only by the user whose wall it belongs to.

To see a good example of a Mahara wall being used, visit the former Mahara core developer Nigel McNie's wall at `http://mahara.org/blocktype/wall/wall.php?id=12`.

Some more profile page examples

Having a look at some other people's profile pages can give you ideas on content and construction. If you go back to `http://mahara.org/user/view.php?id=106` and click on some of Derrin's friends, you can see some more profile pages. Many of them have made their Mahara profile page open to view by the public in just the same way that Derrin has. Other people require you to sign in to Mahara before you view their profile pages.

----- **Punam from Pennytown Primary thinks** -----

All logged in users can see my profile page, so my own learners and also learners and teachers from other schools are going to be able to visit it. I will be able to show off some of the things that interest me, but I don't want to put up too many contact details, I don't want calls from my learners at 11.30 at night.

----- **Janet Norman form PI-Inc thinks** -----

I am going to suggest that all PI Inc users leave their pages available for logged in users only, but I am not going to enforce this because some branch directors may wish their staff to make their profile pages public for some reason or the other. I will definitely be encouraging staff to put up contact details such as their addresses, phone numbers, blog pages, messaging, and conferencing facility usernames, and so on. It will be a useful way of quickly finding out someone's details within Mahara rather than accessing our separate employee database.

As for my own personal profile page, I need to use it to show both who I am and why I am excited about using Mahara as a personalized learning platform, using it to cross international boundaries and bring all of our staff closer together in our working practices.

----- **Neil from Training 4 Work thinks** -----

My profile page will be seen only by students and by other staff members, although some of the clients we provide training for may come and look at it. I am not going to let people view my profile page unless they are logged in. It is there for the learners, really. I think I will populate my own page with contact information for myself and also some basic CV details.

You can do much more with your profile page, though. So, let's start by looking at something we can add.

Adding a text box to your profile page

One useful thing you can add to your profile page, or any View, is a text box. These are extremely useful for giving meaning to your web page. You can use the text box to put in descriptions or snippets of information that help structure your View in a more logical way.

In the next *Time for action* section we look at how exactly you add a text box to your profile page. Along the way, you will encounter for the first time Mahara's drag-and-drop user interface for adding items to Views, which is is very exciting! One of the things that make Mahara stand out is its flexible framework for creating web pages. It is extremely intuitive as you will see, and reflects in some ways how you would create a poster display—taking bits of information such as text and pictures, moving them around until you are happy with their location and then sticking them in place. Of course, the advantage is that, with Mahara, they aren't stuck down forever with glue and can be repositioned whenever you like.

Let's add a text box to our profile View.

Time for action – creating a text box for your profile page

1. Click on the **Edit Profile Page** button in the Profile submenu. You will see a page that looks a bit like this:

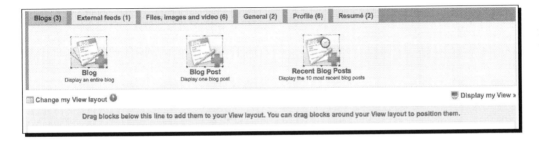

2. You will notice that you are being encouraged to select different blocks from within a set of six tabs at the top of the screen and drag them down onto your View page. Later we will be looking at these blocks and learning how to position them on our page. However, right now we are focusing on how to work with the text box.

   Click into the tab called **General**. You should see this:

3. Click and drag the text box icon somewhere onto the space below to position it amongst the other blocks already on your View layout. You will see the other blocks move as you are dragging to make space for the text box. You will also see a dotted gray line showing you where the new block will appear. Here is a basic diagram showing the drag-and-drop action:

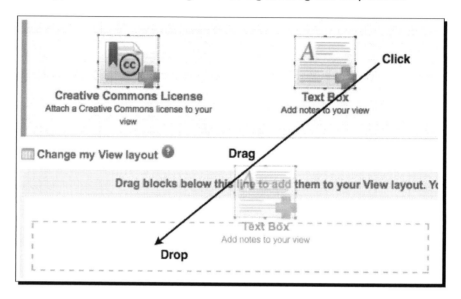

Can't drag and drop in Internet Explorer 6.

The functionality allowing us to drag blocks around the page when we are editing a Mahara View is enabled by JavaScript. Most modern browsers support JavaScript as default, including Firefox, Safari, and Internet Explorer 7 and 8. Unfortunately, many people are still running Internet Explorer 6 and Mahara's drag-and-drop facility won't work in this browser because of problems (or bugs) it has with layout that newer browsers don't. You can still use IE 6 without the drag and drop feature, and use the radio buttons instead, but we recommend you to upgrade your Internet Explorer browser or (even better) download an open source browser such as Mozilla's Firefox: www.mozilla.com/firefox/.

4. A box will open. Click into the **Block Title** and add your title.

5. Click into the **Block Content** box. Type in here the body of your text box. Janet Norman decided that she would like to have some information about Mahara on her profile page.

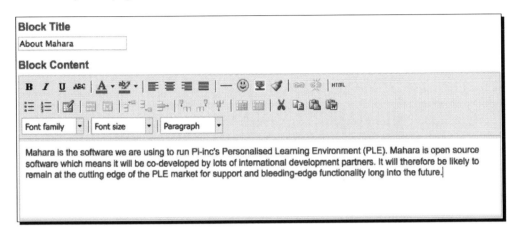

6. Click **Save** to finish and that's it, you've added you first text box.

What just happened?

You just added a text box to your profile page.

A section on your View is called a block, and you've just learned how to add a new text box by clicking and dragging it onto your profile page. Blocks are what Mahara uses to personalize your profile page and your Views. You can add and delete blocks, and move them around. There are actually quite a variety of blocks, and the Mahara developers are keen to keep adding to the list. We have started here with a basic text box, as it's probably the one you will use most frequently. In Chapter 4 we will be exploring what we can do with the other blocks that are already available.

One of the things you probably noticed when adding text to your text box was that you have a number of editing options available. Janet would like to make her text look more interesting, so let's revisit our text box and look at what these options do.

Options in the text editor

You will probably find that you have already used most of the options in the text editor when working in word processing programs. Let's have a quick look at some of the most commonly used options.

Icons	Function
B *I* <u>U</u>	These icons can be used to make your characters bold, italicized, or underlined.
	Align your text to the left, to the center, to the right or justify your text into a square, newspaper-style layout.
	Add bullets or numbers to your lists of text.
HTML	To toggle your page into HTML mode.
	Add a hyperlink to your text.
	Break an existing hyperlink.

Now let's try formatting some of the text you have just entered.

Time for action – editing a text box by adding a hyperlink

1. Open the text block you created earlier for editing. You can do this by clicking on the icon that looks a little bit like a cog at the top of the block.

2. We are going to add a hyperlink to the text. Did you notice that the two link icons are grayed out and unclickable? This is because you can't hyperlink to something before you have highlighted it. Do this by clicking and dragging you mouse over the text you want to hyperlink. Now you should see the two hyperlink buttons in color.

3. Click the **Make Hyperlink** button (the one that looks like a chain) to start creating your hyperlink from the word(s) that are highlighted. Jane has chosen to make a link from the word "Mahara" to the Mahara website. You should see a new dialogue box similar to the one below:

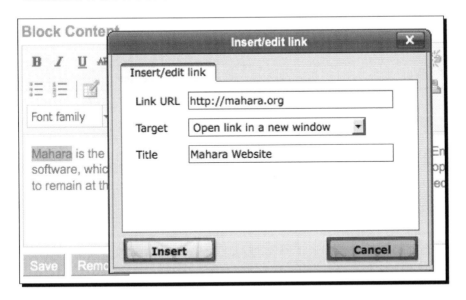

4. You now get the chance to enter your link. Jane therefore enters a link to the Mahara website `http://mahara.org`. She has also added a **Title** to her link. This title displays when the user hovers over the link.

5. Click **Insert**, which will create your link.

6. To finish, remember to click **Save**, otherwise you will lose the work you have just done. You should see the link highlighted in a different color:

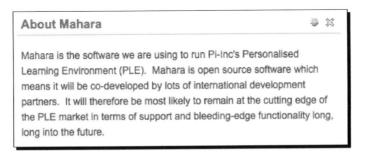

What just happened?

You just edited a text box by adding a hyperlink.

In the last section, we showed you that HTML editing is one of the options in the text editor. Web developers have traditionally used HTML code to write their web pages. It will be useful for regular Mahara users to learn a bit of basic HTML in order to gain more control over their Mahara View pages.

The World Wide Web Consortium offers free, beginner-level HTML tutorials at `http://www.w3schools.com/html/`.

Taking the formatting and editing one step further

Let's now have a look at some of the more advanced options available to you in the text editor.

Icons	Function
A ▾	This allows you to change font color. The drop-down box shows you a set of default colors to choose from and also allows you to choose **More Colors...** from a color picker, from a palette, or even by naming your color with a hexadecimal value.
ab✏ ▾	This drop-down box allows you to set a background color for your text entry. This can be useful for highlighting text or for making header titles, for example.
―	This allows you to add a horizontal ruler to your text box. This can be a really useful way of splitting your text box up into separate sections.
☺	This allows you to add emoticons (more commonly known as "smileys") to your text area. You might be familiar with them from text messages or if you use an instant messenger. Click the button to view the 16 different emoticons you have to choose from. If you hover your mouse pointer over each icon you will be told in words what idea the individual emoticons are trying to express.
✎	Use this to add a table to your text box. You will see that the buttons to the right of this one become colorful once the table is select. Use these to edit the table as you would in a standard word processor.
🖼	This button allows you to display online images in your text box.

Janet has decided on seeing these extra options that her text box needs an image to brighten it up. Let's finish the chapter by seeing how she can do this.

Time for action – adding an image to your text box

1. Find an image on the Internet that you would like to add to your text box. Janet goes straight away to a free images site she knows called "Stock Exchange" at: `http://www.sxc.hu`. She enters the word ePortfolio into the search box and finds some suitable images. She chooses an image of a man jumping in the air with his portfolio in hand.

2. Copy the link to the image. You can usually do this by right-clicking on the image and clicking **Copy image location**.

3. Reopen the text box on your profile page that you made earlier and click the **Insert/edit image** icon.

4. You will see a dialogue box pop up. In the **Image URL** field, paste the location of the image that you copied in step 2.

5. Give your image a relevant **Image description**. This shows when you hover over the image with your mouse cursor.

6. Select the **Alignment, Dimensions, Border**, and **Vertical space / Horizontal space** for your image.

7. When you have finished, click **Insert**. This is how Janet configured her image.

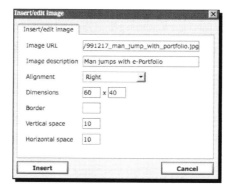

8. You may find that you chose the wrong dimensions for your image. Rather than going back into the image editor by clicking on the image itself and then clicking the **Insert/edit image** button again, you can resize the image in the text editor itself by clicking and dragging the corners to stretch it. Seeing her image on the page itself, Janet decided that she wanted it to be bigger.

What just happened?

We just saw how to add an image to a text box in Mahara.

Why not play around yourself with a few text boxes on your profile page? Have a go at inserting an image into the text box. When you feel you are finished, toggle out of full screen mode and don't forget to click the green button to save your changes when you have finished your editing.

Summary

You have learned a lot in this chapter and really got going with the basics of Mahara. Hopefully, you will now feel like you have a good understanding of some of the basic concepts in Mahara, including your profile information and profile views. We specifically looked at registering onto a Mahara demo site, logging in, navigating, entering profile information, and creating our own profile page.

Now that you've learned about profile pages, let's put some more stuff online using files and blogs, which is the topic of the next chapter.

3

Add Files and Blogs to Your Portfolio

In the last chapter, you got started with Mahara, learning how to register and log in, as well as looking at some of the basics. You also learned how to set up your own Profile. Now we're going to start putting information into our Portfolio and seeing how to add some of this to the Profile Page you made in the last chapter.

In this chapter we shall:

- Learn how to upload files to our Portfolio
- Organize our files using folders and tags
- Start blogging
- Show off our blogs and files on our Profile Page
- Rearrange the layout of our Profile Page

Putting your files online

Before we go into the details of how we put our files into Mahara, let's think over why we want to do this.

Mahara replaces the USB stick

You can log on to Mahara from anywhere if you have access to the Internet, using an Internet Browser. This is great, because it means that you are able to upload and review your files, folders, blogs, and views whenever you need to! Some have described Mahara as an online USB stick, although we have already seen that it is much more than this when we started creating our Profile Page.

Mahara is a central resource space which allows you to share the stuff you put into it. No longer do you need to store all your important files in one place. Soon enough you are going to be presenting your work to others while you are sunning yourself on the beach!

Mahara prides itself on its quick file upload facility, which is the feature we are going to look at first. Let's upload your files into your own private space...

Time for action – adding some folders and files to your Portfolio

1. Click the **My Portfolio** option on the Main Menu. By default, the **My Views** tab will be selected. We will be using this area later to create some more views, but for now, click on the **My Files** tab.

2. We recommend that you start by creating yourself a file structure of folders just as you would do on your laptop or desktop computer. Don't worry about getting them perfect, because you will be able to edit this structure later. Enter the name for your first folder, and click **Create folder**. In the example below, Janet Norman has created a folder in her portfolio called Social:

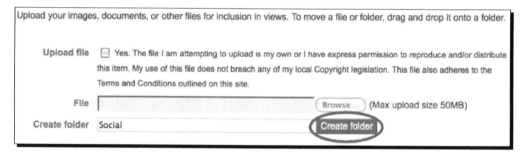

3. You should now see the folder that you have just created. By the side of it you have the options to edit or delete it. Let's add some more details to our new folder by giving it a description. Click the **Edit** button.

4. You will now see a new section appearing below. Write in your description for your folder. This will appear in the information next to the folder under the heading **Description**. When you have finished, click **Save changes**.

5. Go ahead and make as many folders as you like.

6. We're ready to start adding files. Click into one of the folders you just made. You will notice that there is an option at the top of the page called **Upload file**. You will need to check the **Yes** button to agree that the file you are going to upload is yours.

7. Under the **File** option, click **Browse** and search for a file on your own computer that you would like to add to your Mahara Portfolio. Choose the file you want and click **Open**. You will see a spinning progress wheel that is telling you that your file is uploading. Be patient and let Mahara do its work—the larger the file, the longer it takes to upload. When the file has uploaded, the spinning progress wheel will turn into a confident check mark and you will see that your file has appeared in your files area. Below you can see that Janet has uploaded a video of herself talking about her hobbies called 'myHobbies.mov':

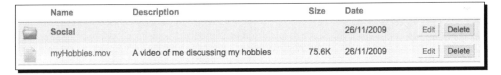

What just happened?

You have just used the **My Files** area of your Mahara site. You have learned how to set up a folder structure and uploaded your first file. In the example, Janet Norman uploaded a video file (.mov), but the file you upload in Mahara can be almost anything: a word-processed document, a spreadsheet, an audio clip, a PDF, and so on.

You may have noticed that when you uploaded your file there was a small message indicating that your file has been uploaded. These helpful messages appear from time to time in Mahara—to close them, just click on the little cross button to the right of the message:

Let's just reflect a little on some of the other things we came across during the file upload process.

Giving structure to your folder tree and branches

Although it is possible to make modifications to your folder structure at any time you wish, it is a good idea to work out how you want to organize your folders right from the very beginning. Here are some options for you to think about:

- You could set up folders by file type. For example: video (mp4, avi, ogv), audio (mp3), doc (odt, odp, ppt, ods, xls), images (png, gif, jpg), and so on.

- You could set up folders by audience (for example, friends, colleagues, finance, sales team, and so on).

- You could set up folders by content or topic (for example, electrics, lathe, cutting, and so on).

- You could set up folders according to commonly known in-house reference codes (for example Class3A, Topic7a(ii), and so on).

- ...or any way you wish.

The key point is that you should try to keep things organized. Later in this chapter we will see how you can use tags to be even more organized.

Copyright

Before you uploaded your file you had to check a box acknowledging that you hold copyright over or have the right to reproduce the material you are about to upload. Legal ownership over files you publish will be your personal responsibility, so please do not upload material you are not allowed to upload. You can always link out to existing material published by other people on the Web if you need to, and we will show you how to do this in the next chapter. But, just to remind you again, you will have the legal responsibility for stuff that you upload into your files area.

Upload limit

In the *Time for action* section, you may have noticed a **Quota** block appearing on the right-hand side of the screen that looked a bit like this:

This useful information tells you how much storage space you have in your site **Quota**. By default, this value is **50.0MB**. You can see in the above example that Janet has used **20.8MB** of her quota, which is **42%** of what she is allowed according to the progress bar. As you upload more files you will notice the progress bar moving across this space to indicate what percentage of your allocated space you have left. Should you feel that you need to have a larger quota allocated to you, get in touch with your Mahara tutor or administrator.

Let's have a look now at how we can edit, delete, and move our files, as well as tagging them.

Moving and deleting files

You will probably enjoy playing around with Mahara's files and folder structure. Wherever you see a folder named **Parent folder**, click into it to jump up to the parent folder. To move files around different folders, just click them and drag them into the folder where you want them to be. Fun isn't it? This facility is similar to the block drag and drop we saw in the last chapter when adding a textbox to our Profile Page. It is powered by JavaScript and is one of the many fun features Mahara has to offer.

To delete a file, simply click on the **Delete** button to the right of it. To the right you will also see an **Edit** button—clicking this button drops down a handy little section that allows you to enter some information for the file:

Try giving your file a **Description** and click **Save changes**.

Uploading more than one file

New to Mahara 1.2 you now have the ability to upload more than one file at a time. This is a great time saver, especially if you have lots of files to add to your Portfolio in one go. Let's see how you can do it.

Time for action – multiple file upload

1. Start by putting all the files you want to upload to Mahara into one folder.

2. Then compress or zip the folder. The resulting zipped folder will end in `.zip`, `.tar`, or `.tar.gz`. How you zip a folder will depend on which operating system you are using but there is plenty of online help to show you how to do this.

3. Upload your newly created zipped folder to a relevant place in your Mahara Portfolios as you would with any other file. You should now see it in your files area.

4. You will see that an **Unzip** button has appeared. Click on it to begin unzipping the folder:

5. The next page will show you the details of your zipped folder, including where the new files will appear in your Portfolio and which files are included in the zipped folder. Click **Unzip** again:

6. The final page shows the unzipping in progress. When it's finished, you will see how many files/folders have been created. Click **Continue** to finish:

7. You will now see that the new folder(s) and files have been added to your Portfolio.

What just happened?

You just learned how to add more than one file at a time to your Mahara Portfolio.

Now let's look at how you can add tags to your files.

Using tagging to organize your files and search for them

"Tags" are a really useful feature and are being increasingly used in modern web technologies. When you tag something, you are giving it a label, which describes something about it. Each tag is a single descriptive "keyword" Tags become useful later on when it comes to searching for items. All files tagged with a certain keyword are grouped together, so they become much easier to locate. Also, you may not want to locate a specific file by name, but to find files within a certain topic area.

As an example, you may know that you have some images of cars in your Mahara files area and would like to find one without knowing the file name. Since you have tagged all the files with the keyword "car", you can search on that keyword and will have a selection of car images to choose from.

Janet chose to tag her video upload with three different tags:

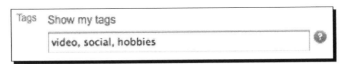

The next time Janet uploads a file, she could choose to click **Show my tags**. She will then see:

She can now see that **hobbies, social**, and **video** have already been used as tags and how many times that has happened. She can select from these tags for her latest file as well as add more new tags underneath. Before long, Janet is going to have a really useful "tagsonomy" or classification system for her files, and do you know what's best of all? When Janet has put up a lot of files in her Mahara site, she will be able to quickly search for her files by entering the tag as a search term into the **Search My Portfolio** block on the right-hand column of her screen.

There is also a very useful **Tags** block, which comes with Mahara 1.2. This block shows you all the most popular tags in your Mahara site. Currently, Janet just has three tags entered:

As a certain tag becomes more popular (because you have tagged more files with the same tag), you will see that the size of the text in your **Tags** block will change to reflect this. The bigger the text, the more popular the tag. Janet has tagged another file as being a video, but it isn't a hobby video, nor is it social. The **video** tag text has changed to show that it is more popular than the other tags:

If you click on any of the individual tags listed in the **Tags** block, you will see a screen where you can manage your tags.

When you have a lot of tags in your Mahara, have a play using this section to search through your tags. You get the choice of doing this both alphabetically and by frequency. You can also edit your tags here.

It might be a good idea to use tags to complement, not replicate, your folder structure. For example, if you organize your folders into file types, it might be a good idea to use your tags to describe subject matter.

----- **Punam from Pennytown Primary thinks** -----

I think I will use my folder structure to first of all distinguish between who the files are for: Pupils, Teachers, Friends. I am then going to split my Pupils folder into the names of all the different class groups I teach. I am going to use the tagging system to group things up according to their content / topics; for example, tudor-clothes, tudor-food, tudor-pastimes, and so on.

Pop quiz – files, folders, and tagging

1. Which feature of Mahara is being described; "A single keyword that describes something about an item such as a folder or file in your portfolio. Useful for helping you to search for items in your portfolio":

    a. Tags

    b. Profile Information

    c. Blogs

    d. Files

2. Think of three different ways that you could use to organize your Mahara folder structure.

3. Does checking the copyright button when uploading a file to Mahara make you legally responsible for that file?

4. If you start running out of quota space in Mahara, whom should you contact to look at getting some more?

Have a go hero – start setting up your files, folders, and tags

It goes without saying that your Mahara ePortfolio will probably become a lifetime project and that you will be making pretty big changes to your files and folders as you progress through your lifelong learning journey. We will see later in the book that a brand new feature in Mahara 1.2 is that you can import/export your data from Mahara platform to Mahara platform (or, indeed, another type of ePortfolio software platform) as you move around between employers and educational institutions.

However, we hope we have helped you to understand that it is a good idea to organize your files, folders, and tags systematically and logically.

Please spend some time now uploading some of your most precious and useful files and then start organizing those files into some sort of sensible structure using folders, file descriptions, and tags.

Blogging

Have you ever blogged? In this section, we are going to learn how to set up blogs and write their corresponding blog posts in Mahara. We are not going to publish these blog posts yet, that will come later.

What is a blog?

The word "blog" derives from the combined words "web" and "log"; that is, "web + "log" = "weBLOG". Think of a "log" as in:

"Captain's log, stardate 43198.7. The enterprise remains in standard orbit ..."

The blog is, in essence, a modern format for a diary. Not everyone in this world chooses to share their reflective diaries with others, but many do.

Seriously, many people get confused into thinking that a blog is a way of communicating online. In fact, a blog is more usefully thought of as an online notepad or diary.

In Mahara we create a variety of blogs and then we use those blogs as a way of collecting our reflective thought processes on different topics. Actually writing things down is a useful process for helping us to understand our thoughts more clearly than we would understand them otherwise. It obviously helps to use different topics, which can organize our thoughts and learning in a neat and ordered way.

Some people do then choose to share these written reflections with others, and Mahara will actually allow us to go public with our blogs, if we choose to. We will see how to do this later in the chapter when we add our blog to our Profile Page. Once you have got the hang of it, Mahara actually offers a really easy way of setting up really attractive public blogs and can be considered a serious contender to many of the other public blogging platforms out there.

So you now know that you should be blogging, let's find out how we can do that in Mahara.

Time for action – creating your first Mahara blog

1. Click into **My Portfolio** in the main menu and then into **My Blogs** in the sub-menu bar of your Mahara. You already have one blog ready for you to used. It will be named according your own name—for example, Neil Martin's blogs.

2. Rather than posting in the default blog, let's start by seeing how to make a brand new one. Click on the button in the top right-hand corner labeled **Add Blog**.

3. Click on the button in the top right-hand corner of the **My Blogs** panel called **Add Blog**.

4. On the next screen, you will have to enter a title and description for your blog. Mahara handily gives you some examples of the kind of titles and descriptions that could be used. You can also add some tags for your blog in just the same way as you added tags for your files earlier on. Go ahead and fill in the information, and when you have finished, click **Create Blog**.

5. You will see your new blog displayed on your **My Blogs** page. Neil has already started making a few blogs in his Mahara, and he can see this:

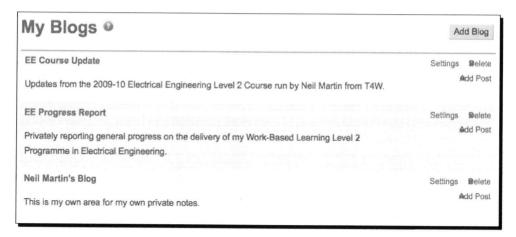

6. Now that we have created our first blog, let's see how we can add posts to it. Click on the name of the blog you created earlier in the far left-hand column. Here you will see a button called **Settings**; click it. This will take you back to the page you first edited when you set up your blog. You will also see the words: **No posts yet. Add one!**. So, let's do just that.

7. Click the **Add Post** button to add post. You will see the familiar options to add title, body, and tags again. Remember that this time you are adding a single blog post. Neil is currently entering a post called **May Report** into his **EE Progress Reports** blog which is aimed at his boss:

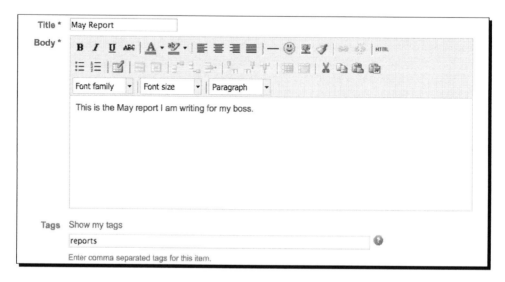

8. Scroll down the page. You will see that you have some more really useful options available here. Click **Add a file** to add a file to your blog from either your hard drive or your Mahara file system.

9. You also have the option to toggle this post as a **Draft** by placing the check mark in the check box. This means that should you choose to allow access to a view containing your blog in the future, this particular post will remain private until you take away that check mark. In this set up, Neil, for example, can work on his monthly report blog posts as and when he wants to but can release them for his boss's view only when he feels they are ready to go. Click **Save post** to finish.

10. After your blog post is published, you will see the date of posting, and you will have the options to edit and delete it later:

| May Report | Published | Edit | Delete |
| This is the May report I am writing for my boss. |

11. As you add posts to your blog, your blog will display the most recent post first.

What just happened?

You just learned to use blogs within Mahara. Later in this chapter, you will be seeing how you can add these to your Profile Page that you started editing in Chapter 2, *Getting Started with Mahara*.

You should now be starting to think about the kinds of blogs that you would like to write. Perhaps you want to write an end-of-week report, which you will want to share with your boss, or with your students. Perhaps you would like to write a funny weekend diary to share with a few of your friends. Perhaps you have a passion—a topic that you want to go public with and share your rants and ramblings with the world. Don't be scared to have a go—nobody needs to look if you don't want them to. Remember this is for you—it doesn't have to be perfect.

We just saw how to create a blog and add posts to it. You have to be careful in Mahara to understand the difference between the two. A blog should be given a more general name, and will contain blog posts related to the subject area. For example, a blog may be entitled "My fitness regime". The blog posts are the individual entries to the blog. A blog entry to the fitness regime blog may be called "Day 1—Gym session".

----- **Neil from Training 4 Work thinks** -----

I mustn't confuse my blogs with my blog posts. A blog contains many posts. Therefore I should not create a blog entitled "May Report"—I should call my blog "EE Progress Reports" and write various posts into that blog called "May Report", "June Report", and so on.

I also need to remember who are the intended audience for my blogs. "EE Progress Reports" is going to be for my boss, so I can write some fairly personal stuff about individual students. "Neil's Notes" is going to be a completely private space for me, I am never going to publish this in a view, so I can write what I like in here. "EE Course Update" is a blog that I am going to publish for my learners to view. I will need to keep what I write in here depersonalized and always upbeat and positive.

Embedding an image in your blog post

We saw in the last *Time for action* section that Neil has made a very simple textual blog post. One great feature of Mahara is that you are able to add audio, video, and images to your blog posts. To do this, when creating your blog post, click on the **Add file** button at the bottom of the blog post creation screen. Then use the **Select** button to select the file to add it to your blog:

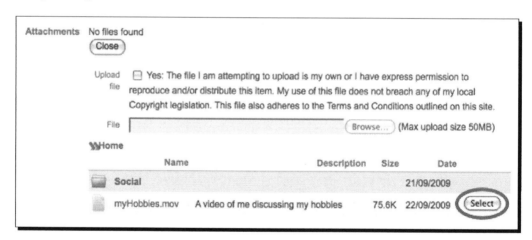

Now that the file has been added to your post, you can use the image upload icon in the body of your post to include the file you just added. You saw how to use this icon in the last chapter. Once you have added the image to your post, you are able to align it and resize it as you wish.

Pop quiz – blogging in Mahara

1. What can a blog be used for?

   A. Reflect on your own experiences

   B. Show other people what you are thinking about

   C. Both of the above.... and more

2. Apart from using simple text blogs what can you do to make your Mahara blogs more attractive?

----- **Punam from Pennytown Primary thinks** -----

My nine-year old pupils aren't really cognitively ready to use blogging as a reflective learning tool. They could use blogs as a way of telling me what work they have done during the week, though. This will encourage them to think more carefully about what they do in their project time in class. It is also a way for me to see whether they are doing their homework activities or not.

----- **Janet Norman form PI-Inc thinks** -----

Blogging will be central to PI Inc work. Not only do we need PI Inc staff to grow by their reflection as they blog, we also need to encourage Knowledge Transfer between people working in similar roles in different branches and in different countries. We will therefore need to get people producing interesting blogs, which they will be publishing for others to read within their different interest groups. We will benefit as an organization if we can encourage our staff to think creatively and to exchange their knowledge! Blogs will facilitate this.

----- **Neil from Training 4 Work thinks** -----

I am blogging for different audiences myself within my Mahara site. I am going to use Mahara to publish a blog on Electrical Engineering topics, which I am going to make public on the World Wide Web and advertise at conferences and in trade journals. I am also going to get my learners writing individual blogs on a weekly basis for me to read in their WBL Evidence views. This way, I can track their individual progress on the course and open up an online channel of communication between me and each and every one of them.

Have a go hero – go on... get reflecting...

As a Personalized Learning Environment, Mahara is very keen to get you reflecting on your learning, and blogs are a key tool for you to use to do that. If you take time to sit down and express what you understand about something in writing, you will generally find that you come out of the experience knowing and understanding more about your topic area than you did before you started.

If you are blogging already, try blogging in Mahara. If you have never blogged before, get started now, you really won't regret it!

Reflecting is one of the most important parts of the portfolio process. Helen Barrett and Jonathon Richter of the University of Oregon have developed a good set of resources on the subject; it's worth a look: `http://sites.google.com/site/ reflection4learning/home`.

We are going to finish this chapter by revisiting our Profile Page.

Linking to files, folders, and blogs in your Profile Page

We saw in the last chapter how you can use textboxes on your Profile Page to convey useful information and to add structure. It will also be really useful to add some links to your files and blogs—you can send somebody a link to your Profile Page, and they will be able to access and read any blog you make available there. The same goes for any files you want to share with other people. So let's see how we can share our stuff with the outside world.

Time for action – linking to files, folders, and blogs in your Profile Page

1. Click the sub-menu tab **Edit profile Page**, which is under the main menu's **Profile** tab.

2. Look at the six different tabs, which contain the blocks ready for you to drag and drop onto the Profile Page you are about to edit. Let's start by adding a file that visitors to our Profile Page can download. Click the **Files, images and videos** tab.

3. Drag the **File(s) to Download** block into your Profile View.

4. You will see a dialogue box open. Remember we added some files earlier? Told you those files would come in useful! Here you can add a file from your Portfolio, or quite handily, Mahara allows you to upload a new file into your profile from this block's interface. Choose the file to add, and click **Select**. You will see your file has now moved to the top, listed under the **Files** label.

5. Continue selecting all the files you would like to add until you are happy. Note that you can use the **Remove** button to the right of a file at any point to remove it from the selection. To finish, click **Save**. Janet Norman adds her **myHobbies** movie to her Profile Page to share with people:

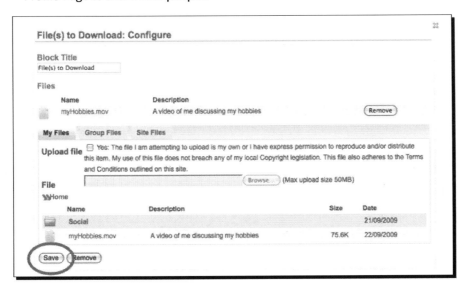

6. You can now see your file on your Profile Page available as a download.

7. Now click and drag in the **A Folder** block. Do you remember creating folders to put your files in? You can make a folder from your files area available on any one of your view pages, including your Profile Page. This will make it possible for your audience to download any of the files that are available in that folder. If you have several files, this will be much faster than using the **File(s) to Download** block several times. Try selecting a folder and adding it to your Profile Page.

8. Click on the first tab called **Blogs**. Remember those blogs you started creating earlier? You will now insert them into your Profile View so that others can view them.

9. You will see that you have three options. You can add an entire blog with all its posts, a single blog post, or a list of the 10 most recent blogs posts:

10. Let's add the single blog post we made earlier. Click and drag the **Blog Post** block onto your Profile Page. In the box that opens, add a title to your block if you wish to. Then, click on the radio button next to the blog post you want to select, and then click **Save**.

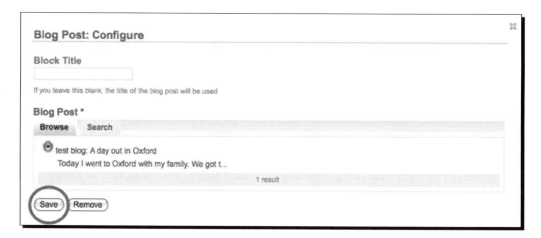

11. Hey presto, your blog post has now been placed in your Profile Page automatically! Try doing the same with the **Blog** and **Recent Blog Posts** blocks.

What just happened?

You've learned how to add files to download in your Profile Page. Adding a file to a view is a quick way of giving people access to that file. Obviously, the person opening the file needs to have the computer program to open the attachment the other end. This is sometimes the reason why it is better to embed an image or video into your site, then they can view it in Mahara without the need for the person to download it and then find a program to open it with. We will be looking at how to do this in the next chapter.

We also added a blog post to our Profile Page. Remember, you are allowed to display an entire blog, a single blog post, or the last ten posts that you wrote. Remember, if you have checked any of your recent blog posts as being "draft only", these blog posts will not be displayed here. Mahara gives you these options, as it is often preferable to display the most recent, or last post, rather than displaying an entire blog, some of which could contain scores or even hundreds of blog posts. You will notice that in this third type of blog display block you are given a drop-down list asking you to determine if other people can copy this element of your view or not. Think about whether you want people to copy your blog or not. As you can link to other blogs and feeds outside Mahara, maybe you would like the world to do the same, or maybe you want to keep this blog as an internal one. The choice is yours. We will talk all about view copying and templating in the next chapter.

----- **Punam from Pennytown Primary thinks** -----

I am going to make a folder viewable later for my students—not in my Profile Page but in another view that I will set up as an introduction to our course. In this folder I am going to make available all the handwritten worksheets my students have to fill in by hand. They can then download these worksheets onto their own computers and either edit them in their word processors or print them out and write onto them before handing their work back to me. I can see this working very well.

----- **Janet Norman form PI-Inc thinks** -----

It will be a great idea for me to display the last ten posts from my "PLE Developments" blog on my profile page. Members of the international PI-Inc Mahara community are going to be keen to keep up to date with the developments surrounding our new online Mahara space. If my blog is there for all registered users to see on my profile page it will be the easiest thing in the world for people to pop by and catch up with important changes and events.

----- **Neil from Training 4 Work thinks** -----

My job-seeking learners can make a PDF version of their CVs available for download from their own profile pages for potential employers. I am looking forward to learning how to set up some specialist group views in Chapter 5, because I can then put all of the important course documentation into one of the views ready for the learners to access and download. There are no files I want to make downloadable from my Profile Page, though. Not at the moment, anyway...

Summary

We learned a lot in this chapter about how we can add files, folders, and blogs to our Portfolio. We also learned about how to tag things in your Portfolio.

We discussed how we might use these different tools in the different learning contexts represented by our three fictional case studies. Hopefully, you now appreciate some of the values of blogs, goal-setting, and skills-appreciation as useful reflective learning tools.

Finally, we added some of our stuff (files/folders, and blogs) to our Profile Page. We are now ready to learn more about views and start adding some stuff to our views that we can show to other people. That is the topic-area of the next chapter.

4
Views

In the last few chapters, you have learned about your Profile Page, Files, and Blogs. You saw how we can add our Profile Information, Files, and Folders to our Profile Page using some of the blocks provided. You learned that your Profile Page is actually a special type of View in Mahara. In this chapter, you are going to find out more about Views and what you can do with them. You will see how standard Views differ from your Profile Page including which extra blocks you have to choose from. We will also look at how to control who has access to our Views.

In this chapter, we shall:

- ◆ Create a new View from scratch
- ◆ Share our View with others
- ◆ Limit the length of time we allow access to our View
- ◆ Create a copyable View
- ◆ Copy a View from someone else's portfolio
- ◆ Look at a best practice example—multi-page Views
- ◆ Look at a guide for assessing the quality of your Views

What are Views in Mahara?

In Chapter 2, *Getting Started with Mahara*, we introduced the concept of being able to create "web pages" in Mahara, which we call Views. You also got a glimpse of how easy it is to use the drag-and-drop facility of View in order to add blocks to a View when tailoring your Profile Page.

Views are great! They are one of the stand-out features of Mahara and we think you are really going to enjoy learning to use them. Views, like blogs, are an excellent tool for reflection. The difference between the two is that a blog is very text orientated with a user reflecting on a topic in writing (with usually an odd image or video to supplement the text), but Views allow you to express your ideas in more of a "web page" type format using lots of different blocks. Also, Views are flexible; you can very easily add and remove whichever blocks you want.

You can include a variety of items in your View such as text, images, profile information, and even blogs. When you have done that, you can rearrange them how you wish by changing the View layout.

Not only can a View be used for personal reflection on a topic, but Views are also great for presenting information to others. You can control access to your Views, meaning you get to decide who sees your Views and when. Let's think about some of the things you can do with Views in Mahara:

- You could present all of your ideas related to one of the topics in a qualification you are taking. This could be for your own reference or you may choose to share access to this View with your tutor or classmates.

- You could use a View to take notes on all of the thoughts, ideas, links, and so on, that you gather while you are attending a conference (if you have a wireless connection). You can then share the View with your colleagues after the event to show them what you have learned.

- You could use a View to explore and express your thoughts on a particular aspect of your social or family life, such as a family holiday. This is likely to be private, and something you would only share with other members of your family.

- You could use a View as a tutor to present all of the important materials your learners need to read, watch, listen to, and think about in preparation for a particular topic they are going to study with you. Lots of lecturers prefer to use Mahara to present their work instead of doing so in a Virtual Learning Environment such as Moodle. This may be partly because the lecturer's name (and avatar) will continue to be associated with the work presented in the Mahara View even after they retire or move on to another academic institution.

- You could use a View to present an ongoing progress report on a project you are doing at work. You might make a blog post an element of this View as well as make important files related to your project available for sharing.

These are just a few examples, but of course there are potentially hundreds of different things that you could use a Mahara View to achieve.

There are three stages to View creation. Let's see the first stage of this process; how we can create a View from scratch and add content to it.

Time for action – creating and laying out your View

1. To create a View from scratch, click on the **My Portfolio** area on the Main Menu bar.

2. Now click on the **My Views** tab. You should see a screen similar to Punam's below; she has decided she is now going to create a View about the Tudors. You will see that you currently have no Views listed in this area:

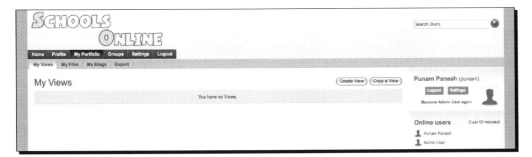

3. Click the **Create View** button on this page.

4. The screen you now see is almost identical to the one that you saw when creating your Profile Page; however, the title is different—**Create View Step One: Layout**. From the title, you can probably guess that there is going to be more than one step. In this *Time for action* section, we will be concentrating on this first step. You will notice that no blocks have been automatically added for you:

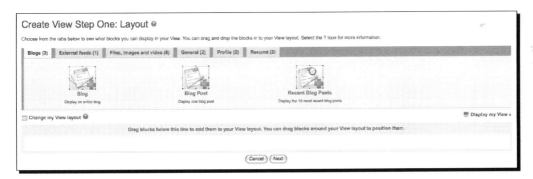

5. Punam decides to start creating her first View on 'The Tudors'. She remembers that the text block hides under the **General** tab. Drag a **Text Box** into your View. Punam uses her textbox to write an introduction to her View:

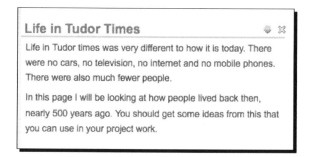

6. She then decides that she wants to add an image to her View. To add an image, click on the **Files, images and video** tab.

7. Drag the **An Image** block into your desired position on the page and fill in the settings in order to link to an image stored in your Files area or upload a new image. This is what Punam's View now looks like:

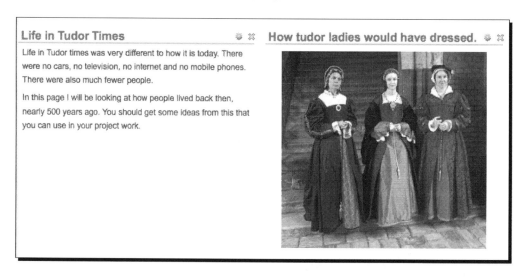

8. Finally, Punam decides to add a video to her View. You will find the videos block under the **Files, images and video** tab. We are going to add a video from the popular video sharing website, **YouTube** (http://youtube.com). Start by dragging the **External Video** block into your View.

9. You will then see a pop-up box with options for this block. Before you enter your settings here, you will need to navigate to an external video site and choose a video that you like. This doesn't have to be YouTube; you could also choose Google videos (`http://video.google.co.uk`), Teacher Tube (`http://teachertube.com`), or SciVee (`http://scivee.tv`). Search for a video that you would like to add to your View. When you have found it, copy the URL from either the address bar or from the link provided with the video.

10. Punam has found a video from a 'Horrible Histories' Series on YouTube. On the settings page, enter the URL in the **Video URL** section. Then choose a **Height** and **Width** for your video in pixels. The standard 250 x 250 is usually fine. When you've finished, click on **Save**:

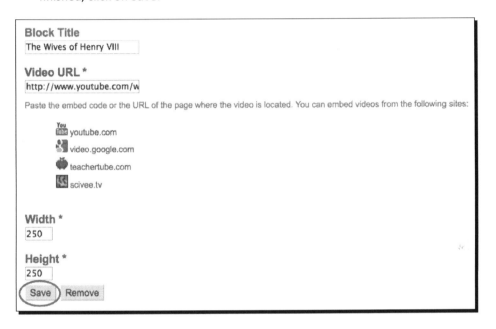

11. Her View now looks like this:

12. On seeing her View, Punam decides the she would like the video to be in the middle column and the image to be in the right-hand column.

13. You can move blocks around the page using the same drag-and-drop method that you used to add them. Click on the title of the block and try dragging it around the View. You will see how the other blocks move to make space and a dotted box appears to show you where it will be positioned:

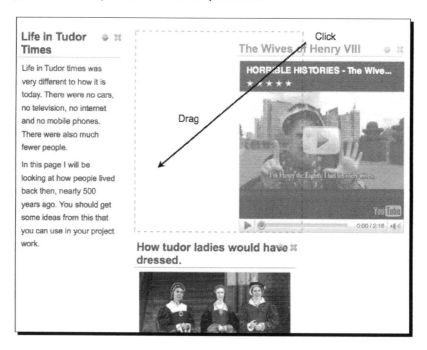

14. Punam drags her blocks into the correct position and her View now looks like this:

15. That's all there is to creating a new View, adding blocks, and rearranging them.

What just happened?

We just saw where we can go to make Views in Mahara, had a go at adding some blocks, and learned how to rearrange the blocks on the page.

You will have noticed that there are a few differences between the Profile Page and other Views too. The blocks are all the same with the exception of the wall block, my views block and my groups block, which are only available in your Profile Page. However, virtually everything else to do with creating, editing, and manipulating blocks around your View is identical. If you feel like learning a bit more about the blocks available to add to your View, look for the section called *Blocks*, which appears later in this chapter.

Any time you want to see your View while you are editing it, just click on **Display my View** on the layout editing page:

This will show you what you View will look like to a user. The only difference between what you see and what a user sees is that you will also see a bar at the top of the page. Use this bar to go **Back** or **Edit** to return to the editing page:

Unlike editing your Profile Page, creating a View is a three step process. This is useful as you can come back to each of these steps later and edit them individually without having to go through the whole three-step process each time. We haven't finished with Views yet; just had a look at the first step of View creation. There is one more thing to mention in the first step—changing your View layout.

Adding/removing columns from your View

Punam is happy that she has managed to add some blocks to her View, but this has also made her think that she would like to give it more structure. She would like to have four columns so that she can associate each column with the following topics:

1. **Column 1**: Introduction and general information such as homework assignments/quiz questions.

2. **Column 2**: Politics of Tudor Britain, that is simple facts about Kings and Queens, Wars, Battles, and so on.

3. **Column 3**: Culture, that is Fashion, Music, Theatre, and so on.

4. **Column 4**: Welfare, that is Housing, Punishment, Food, and so on.

Time for action – changing your View layout

1. To add/remove columns from your View, click on the link below the blocks area called **Change my View layout**.

2. You will now see a screen inviting you to change the **Number of Columns** in your View. You can select between 1 and 5 columns. Punam changes her View to have **4** columns and clicks on **Next**:

3. The final page asks you whether you would like to change your View to have **Larger center columns** or **Equal widths**. Punam decides she would like to stick to equally sized columns and clicks **Change my View layout** to finish:

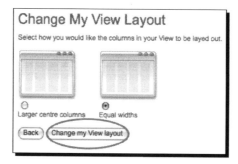

4. Punam's View looks like this with one extra column:

5. Now that you have returned to the View layout screen, click on **Next** at the bottom to move on to the next stage.

What just happened?

You have just changed the layout of your View by adding an extra column and finished the layout step of View creation. We will see how you can return to this page later in order to re-edit your View.

How many columns you add to your View depends on the content you want to add—with there being a maximum of 5 to choose from. Punam has a clear idea about the kind of information she wants to put in each column. You may decide that you want your View to be simpler and only have two columns. This may be important if you are just showing images, for example, and you want them to be as big as possible.

We mentioned in the *Time for action* that you have a choice of having large center columns in your View. This is what Punam's View would have looked like with larger center columns:

Notice how the left-hand column is now squashed to be smaller than the two center ones. This could be useful, for example, if you would like the main information in the center with small images or web links in the side columns. We will be using this format later in the chapter in our example for making a multi-page View.

Now, let's move on to stage two of View creation.

Time for action – adding View details

1. You should already be on the page to begin stage two of View creation. You will see that the title is **Create View Step two: Details**. Start by giving a title to your View. You may have to search for your View later, so remember to make your title relevant to the content.

2. Next, give your View a description and add some tags. These tags work in the same way as the tags you added to your files in Chapter 3, *Add Files and Blogs to Your Portfolio*. Remember they make it easier for you to search for your View later on, so it is worthwhile taking the time to fill them in.

3. Finally, choose a display name. You can decide whether or not to show your First name, Last name, Full name, or Display name. This name appears at the top of your View. Punam decides to choose just her **First name**:

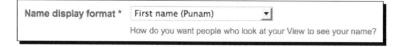

4. Click on **Next** to finish the second step of View creation.

What just happened?

You have just added some important details to your View, including the title, description, tags, and display name. The description section is a really useful way of saying something important about your View before someone has even clicked on it.

Make your View description attractive

Users can get a brief impression of what your View is about by reading the description when they are searching for Views. It is a good idea to make this as attractive and descriptive as possible. Give an introduction to what you will be talking about in the view. Imagine your description to be a snippet from the front page of a newspaper; you want to summarize the most important facts from your View but also make it interesting so that people want to read on. Including an image in the description is one way of making the View more attractive.

Let's move to the final stage of View creation—Access.

View access

So you have made your View and given it some details, but there is still one very important thing to do—decide who gets to see it!

One of the beauties of Mahara is just how much flexibility it gives you over controlling access to your information. You can specify who gets to see what and when.

Time for action – editing your View access

1. You should now be on a page called something like **Edit Access for View "The Tudors"**. Obviously your View will be called something different. Read the information at the top of the page to familiarize yourself with what access means and what we will be doing in this stage.

2. One of the first options you will notice at the top of this page is the **Allow copying** checkbox. This allows others to copy your View. Leave this option unchecked for now.

3. The middle section is about allowing access. To the left of the page are all the people or groups of people you can allow access to and to the right are those people who can access your View. Currently you will see that there are no people on the right-hand side:

4. To add a group of users, click on the **Add** button next to that set of users:

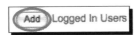

5. You will now see that the user group you selected has moved to the right-hand side under the **Added** label. Punam has decided that she doesn't want to allow access to all logged in users, just to limit it to those who are in her class. Click on **Remove** to remove access for the user group:

6. You can add individual users in the same way that you add groups of users. Search for the user you would like to add and click on **Add**.

7. You will notice that when you add a user, you also get **From** and **To** boxes. This allows you to set a time period for that user to access the View. Enter **From** and **To** dates between which your users can access the View.

8. Finally, at the bottom of the page, you will see that you have the ability to add an **Overriding Start/Stop Date**. This allows you to set a start and stop date for people accessing your View. It will supersede any **From** or **To** dates that you have set.

Use the calendar!

Whenever you can add a date of any description in Mahara, you will see that there is a small calendar to the right of the input box. Usually, this is a quicker way of adding a date than typing it manually because it will enter the date in the correct format for you. You can also see the dates available in the future. This can help in deciding which dates you need to choose by seeing which day of the week they fall on.

9. When you are happy with who you have allowed access to and when they can see your View, click on **Save**.

What just happened?

You have just learned how to make your View copyable, how to allow different groups or individuals to access your View, and setting when those people can access your View.

That was quite a lot to get to grips with, so let's have a look at those stages in more detail now.

Making a View copyable

You saw that Mahara has a checkbox that you can select in order to allow your View to be copied by those who can View it. This function can be useful in a variety of settings. You might want your colleagues to be able to copy your View. Suppose you wanted to create several similar Views, on different topics, but wanted to keep a similar presentational theme for all of them. Rather than checking back constantly to see how you set up the first one, checking this box will allow you to copy the first View, (and as we will see later) rename it, and edit it. This is much quicker than setting up several Views from scratch.

----- Punam from Pennytown Primary thinks -----

I really like this copying facility. All the teachers in our school are really good at working together and collaborating on ideas. Stewart has expressed an interest in our Tudors project, but thinks it might be too young for his sixth grade. I'm going to permit copying so he can copy my View and edit it so that he can put links with handouts that are more relevant for his sixth-grade group.

Naming copyable Views

It is sometimes a good idea to make it obvious in the title of a View that it is copyable. This way both you and other users will know that the View is copyable. One way you could do this is by calling your View a "Template". For example, Punam may call her Tudors View—"Template: The Tudors".

When somebody copies your View, they take over some of the artefacts (files, blogs) that you have created, but this doesn't have to be the case. You may notice that if you have made your View copyable, then you have some more options for each block that you add:

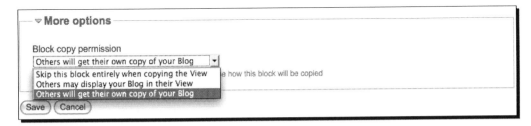

You can decide whether or not a block gets skipped when somebody copies the View. You may, for example, not want the copier to copy your blog. The extra options you have available are to:

1. **Skip this block entirely when copying the View**: The block won't be copied.

2. **Others may display your Blog in their View**: The blog will be displayed, but linked to from your own file area.

3. **Others will get their own Copy of your Blog**: The whole blog and its contents will be copied to the file area of the person who makes the copy.

Deciding who can access your View

One of the beauties of Mahara is just how much flexibility it gives you over controlling access to your information. You can specify who gets to see what and when.

There are four "global" settings, and then you can also specify the users individually:

1. **Public**: Choosing this option will allow your View to be seen by **everyone** whether logged in or not, very much like a public facing website. Sometimes your administrator might leave this option switched off.

2. **Logged in Users**: This will allow your View to be seen by everyone who is a member of the Mahara site and logged in.

3. **Friends**: This will allow access to everyone you have as a friend. You will learn about friends in the next chapter. This is a useful option if you would like to share a View that is only relevant to people who know you within the Mahara site.

4. **Secret Url**: Use this if you would like to give some people who aren't already members of the Mahara site access to your View. The URL is simply a link to the View, which you can set up as a hyperlink in another web page, in a blog, or e-mail so that others can open it. The URL that is created is difficult to guess so that the general public can't see your View. Rather than use it as a hyperlink, you could just send the whole link to the people you would like to give access to the View by pasting it into an e-mail, for example. You will see the URL appear when you add the Secret URL access option:

Curious searchers are not really going to guess `http://pi-inc.tdm.info/View/View/php?t=C2g4JxuhrZMLQA2epTUq` by accident, are they? This is why we can consider this URL to be a secret one.

----- Neil from Training 4 Work thinks -----

I think the secret URL will be useful to our learners. I can see them using it to give potential employers and work placements access to Views containing their CVs and assessed work, without it being available to the public in general. I know that if they present digital (online) CVs, it really improves their chances of success in getting a job as it really makes them stand out from the crowd. They could not only put up their resume information but also display video clips of themselves in action in the workplace, audio clips of their tutors talking about the good progress they have made and recommending them as employees, still images showing some of the work they have completed, and so on. Who wants to present an old-fashioned paper-based CV when you could go digital?

We saw that you can choose people individually but what we didn't mention is that you can also choose to add access in groups. Even though we haven't learned about groups yet, you should see that allowing a group of users access to your View could be very useful. To do this, on the **Edit View Access** page in the section that allows you to search for users, select **Groups** (1) from the drop-down box. Then click on the Magnifying glass o the right-hand side (2). You will now see all the groups that you are allowed to assign access to (3). Here are the groups that Janet can assign to any of her Views:

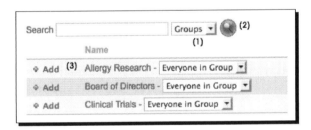

If you have lots of users or groups, it might be easier to type their name or part of the name into the search box and get Mahara to search for you. Another thing to notice is that you can limit access for that group to different roles, including the "Admin" and "Member" roles. Don't worry too much about that now, we will find out what all that means in Chapter 7, *Institution Administrators, Staff Members, and Group Tutors.*

Time-limiting access

We showed you how you can date-restrict access to certain users, but you may have also noticed that when you add a date from the calendar a 24-hour time period also appears. Use this to set the access time to a specific minute of the day you have chosen:

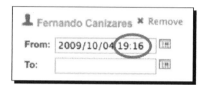

A tutor may use this feature to set up a "Read, Memorize, and Reproduce" activity in a classroom, for example. This activity could give the learners, for example, 15 minutes to read about a particular topic before they go on to recall as much as they have read about the topic as possible, going on to re-present what they have learned to other people in the class who have read different Views.

Another great feature is that you can add a user more than once and give them two different access slots. This may be useful if there are two parts of a course and you would like a break in between so that you can rearrange the View for the second part of the course. Perhaps you would like to add answers to a View that posed some questions to a learner.

> **Using the calendar more efficiently**
>
> Rather than using your mouse to scroll through the months of the calendar to select an appropriate day, you can use the directional arrow buttons on your keyboard. When you are positioned over the correct day, press the *Enter* key and that day will be set as the **To** or **From** access date.

Finally, we also saw how you can set an overriding time. Remember, **this takes priority** over the access times set for individuals or groups.

----- **Punam from Pennytown Primary thinks** -----

I am going to give the student teacher I am helping, Lizzie, access to my View for a week. I want her to be able to see it and get some ideas about how she may make her own View later on. Once she has some ideas for the kind of content she should add, she can start making her own Views from what she has seen.

I also want to limit the dates within which my group of learners are going to be able to access the View. Once I know how to make groups, I will revisit my View and set the access and time limits for my group.

----- **Neil from Training 4 Work thinks** -----

I really see this idea working for our learners. We have some people outside of our institution who need to verify a selection of learner work. I don't really want these "verifiers" to have long term access to the Views. Also, if you have given them access just before and after the visit, they won't get confused by seeing lots of Views that they don't need to see in later visits.

Pop quiz – creating a View

1. Which block is available in your Profile Page but not in a standard View?
2. Which has priority, the access times you set to an individual, or the overriding time?
3. What is a secret URL?
4. Can you give access to more than one person or group?
5. Can you remove access once it has been granted?

Editing your View once you have created it

The View that you created will now have appeared in the **My Views** area of your portfolio. There are three links that appear, which allow you to edit each of the three steps in View creation. They are to:

1. **Edit View details** (1): This relates to step 2 of View creation that we did earlier, where you can change the name or description of your View as well as assigning tags and designing what format your name is displayed in.
2. **Edit this View** (2): Takes you to the important step 1, which allows you to add blocks and rearrange them on your View.
3. **Edit View access** (3): Relates to step 3—who is allowed to see your View and when.
4. You can also **Delete this View** (4).

Punam's View along with its description is as follows:

The Tudors

(4)
Delete this View

Edit View details **(1)**

Want to know more about the tudors? Find out about Henry VIII and his six wives, what people used to wear and how they used to live. There are some fun tudor games too!

Edit this View **(2)**

Artefacts: tudorladies.jpg,

Edit View access **(3)**

Who can see this View: logged in users, Terry Phelps, Copying is allowed

Now that you know how to go back and change things, try to:

- Change the title
- Add a new block
- Change access rights

You can use the block descriptions in the next section to make a choice about which new block you would like to add. Try adding one that you haven't used before to see what you can achieve.

Blocks

So far, we have seen a few of the blocks that are available to you to add to your View, including the "Text Box", "Profile Information", and "An Image" blocks. Here is a breakdown of all the blocks that are available in Mahara 1.2 and what you might use them for:

Category	Name	Image	Description
Blog	Blog		Use this block to display your entire blog. All the postings from the blog are shown in the block.
			If you are blogging on a certain subject, you may want to use Mahara to show other people your reflections. You could display your whole blog in a View and make it publicly available. People will then be able to give you feedback on what you are saying.
	Blog Post		This shows a single post from a blog. In the block options, you can choose the post you would like to display.
			If you are making Views on a specific topic, you may remember that one of your postings is relevant. Include the post to show your own reflections on the subject.
	Recent Blog Posts		Rather than displaying the whole blog, you can use this block to display the 10 most recent posts.
			You may feel that you want to show updates from your blog, but not the whole thing because previous postings are a bit outdated. If so, this is the block you should use.

Category	Name	Image	Description
External Feeds	External Feed		This block allows you to display valid RSS or ATOM feeds from other websites. You have the choice of whether or not to show a summary of the feed items, or to show their descriptions as well.
			Your View may be an analysis of current trends, for example, in global climate conditions. By including RSS feeds to weather stations/meteorological sources, you are keeping your View up-to-date without having to alter the content yourself.
Files, images and Video	External Video		Use this to link to a video from an external website. In the configuration settings, enter the URL link to the video you want to include in your View. You can embed videos from:
			• YouTube (youtube.com) • Google videos (video.google.com) • Teacher Tube (teachertube.com) • SciVee (scivee.tv)
			You are able to set a width and height for the videos that you embed.
			Videos make your View more interesting. You could include a short educational clip from any of the four sites listed above to exemplify and support any other content in your View.
	File(s) to Download		This allows you to add files to your View that can be downloaded by people. You can allow people to download files from your own files area as well as group files and site files.
			You may have lots of files that you want to share with others. Why not turn your View into a file sharing space where you can allow other people to download files such as PDF files, documents, or images?

Category	Name	Image	Description
	An Image		Use this block to display a single image from your Mahara files area. You can set a width for your image and decide whether or not to show its description. You can also choose group or site images to put in your View. An image makes a View more appealing.
	Embedded Media		Using this, you can display your own media files (video/audio) in your View. Simply choose the file that you would like to embed and give it a width and height. Record your own audio podcast and add it to your files area. You can then add a short snippet of you discussing topics relating to your View. This can often get a message across much better than using a textbox.
	A Folder		Use this to display a single folder. People will be able to see all the files or folders that are contained in this folder. By adding a folder you can allow other people to download lots of files rather than using the File block.
	Some HTML		You can add an HTML file to your View from your files area. If you know the basics of coding HTML, this allows you to add something more bespoke to your View that you wouldn't get using the other blocks. Visit http://www.htmlcodetutorial.com/ for an introduction to HTML coding.
General	Creative Commons License		You can use this to add a Creative Commons License to your View. The license is displayed as a small image. With this, you can indicate whether or not you 'Allow commercial uses of your work' or 'Allow modifications of your work'. If you would like to know more about Creative Commons licensing, visit http://creativecommons.org/
	Text Box		With this, you can add a block of text to your View. You can format the text how you wish, changing layout, color, and so on.

Category	Name	Image	Description
Profile	Contact Information		Use this to display Contact Information that you entered into your Profile. You are allowed to choose exactly what information to display and have the option to hide your e-mail address if you would like to.
	Profile Information		Use this to display Profile Information from your Profile. You can use this to display your Profile Icon if you wish. You also have the option to enter an introduction to your Profile Information.
Resume	Your Entire Resume		With this, you can display the whole of your Resume. All sections, including Personal Information, Employment History, Cover Letter, and so on will be displayed.
	One Resume Field		Use this to display just one field from your Resume. Only the fields that you have already completed in your Resume will be available to include in your View.

Copying Views

We learned earlier how to make our own Views copyable, but how about if we want to copy somebody else's View into our own portfolio? The ability to copy someone's View is a really useful thing. This feature is all about saving time and sharing ideas.

----- Neil from Training 4 Work thinks -----

I think the ability to copy other people's Views will be really helpful for my assessors and learners. I want to create a template View for my assessors, which will contain all the blocks that the learners need to submit their evidence with. It'll make life much easier if each assessor can copy the template for each of their students rather than starting from scratch. As the learners gain confidence, they can learn how to change things around later.

Time for action – copying a View

1. Return to the **My Views** section of your portfolio. Click on the button called **Copy a View**:

2. You will now see a page showing all the Views that you are able to copy in the Mahara site. You can use this page to search for Views by both name and owner. Search for and find the View you would like to copy.

3. Punam has found the View she would like to copy. It is called **The Vikings** and was created by Stewart. She wants to copy it to use the videos included, but wants to add some more textboxes to make it relevant to her older learners. To copy the View, she clicks on **Copy View**:

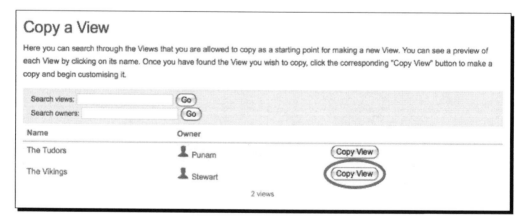

4. You will then be taken to the screen that allows you to re-edit the View, should you wish to, and see a message indicating how many blocks and artefacts (files, blogs, and so on) were copied. On the details page you will see that your View now has a prefix "copy of" in its name—decide whether you would like to keep this.

5. None of the access rights have been copied, so decide who you would like to give access to the copied View.

6. When you have finished, **Save** the View and it will appear in your **My Views** area.

What just happened?

You have just copied a View. This is a really useful feature if you wish to create consistency between Views, either for you personally, or between different staff members. Also, if you have someone new to Mahara, it may be really helpful to provide a template View for them to copy in order to get them started. As an assessor, you may wish to create a template View for your learners to copy with a variety of sections, and then just ask them to populate the various sections with their evidence. We will be seeing more about this in Chapter 7.

You may have noticed that when you were searching for Views to copy, some of your own Views appeared. This is because you have the ability to copy all of your own Views, whether they have been made copyable or not.

Also, when you copied the View, there may have been some files or blogs that were also copied. These will now have appeared in your own file and blog areas. Copied files are all put into a new folder called **viewfiles**:

Blogs are renamed with the "Copy of" prefix. As we saw earlier, blogs and other artefacts may not always be copied depending on how the copyable View has been set up.

Pop quiz – copying Views

1. Once you have copied a View, can you tell the difference between that and a standard View?

2. When you copy a View which parts aren't copied?

View feedback

This is a great feature of Mahara. You have the ability to give feedback on any View that you have access to. This might be useful in the following situations:

♦ You might have asked a peer for feedback on some work you are doing on a particular course in exchange for feedback you can give on their work.

♦ A tutor may have added your View to their Watchlist (see Chapter 6, *Site Settings and Exporting Your Portfolio* for a more detailed discussion on Watchlists). You may then get some informal feedback from your tutor on your work before you submit it for formal assessment (see more on formal assessment in Chapter 7).

♦ You could be using the feedback functionality as a communication vehicle. You may raise a topic for discussion with your workmates, for example, and get them to answer the core question(s) posed in your View by using the feedback option.

♦ You may have used a View to share highlights of a recent holiday experience with your friends in Mahara. They could then use the feedback option to tell you how jealous they are of your rich experiences or at least of your suntan!

The feedback that you give can be both "Private" and "Public" (although your public feedback may have been turned off by the Site Administrator). When you send Private feedback, the feedback is sent to the person who created the View; nobody else can see it. With public feedback, all users can see the feedback and it will appear at the bottom of the View. Any public feedback that is submitted is public unless and until the person who owns the View decides to make it Private.

So, let's now look at the process for giving feedback on a View.

Time for action – feedback on a View's content

1. Start by finding the View that you would like to give feedback on and open it.

2. At the bottom of the page you will see a section with four options listed. Click on **Place feedback**:

3. You will see a box open below. Enter the **Message** that you would like to send to the person who owns the View.

4. By default, the **Make public** option is unchecked. Make your first feedback public.

5. When you are happy, click on **Place feedback**. Stewart from Schools Online has found Punam's View and decided he would like to give it some public feedback:

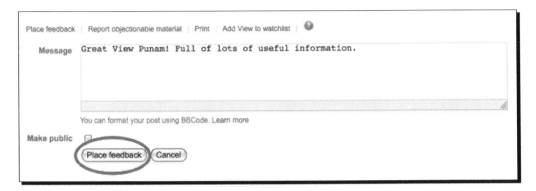

6. You will now see the feedback displayed at the bottom of the View:

What just happened?

You just gave feedback on somebody else's View content. It is important to think carefully about what you are going to write to the person, especially if your feedback is for a learner and has a critical tone. You don't want people to be offended by your comments; be constructive—you want them to feel reassured. You should certainly think carefully before making the feedback public. It is advised that you only make positive and enthusiastic feedback public, otherwise the user is likely to take offence and instantly make it private.

We just saw how to give feedback, but what about the other three options that were listed? This is what else you can do with a View:

- ♦ **Report Objectionable Material**: If you see anything on the View that is "objectionable" or offensive to you, then you can report it to the Site Administrator. Only do this if you are sure the content is offensive. Remember users don't always manage the content of external links, so if the content of an external link is objectionable, it may not always be the user's fault—in this case, check with the user first.

- ♦ **Print**: This gives you a printout of the View.

- ♦ **Add View to Watchlist**: By adding a View to a Watchlist, you can get regular updates about when it has been changed. This is useful for following Views that you found interesting. Whenever the user adds more information you will find out and can then revisit the View.

We have seen how to place feedback. Let's now look at responding to feedback placed on your own View. Punam has now found the feedback that Stewart placed at the bottom of her View. She decides that because the students will see the View, she doesn't want any public feedback to be there, however glowing it may be! You will see that for any feedback placed on your View, there will be a **Change to Private** button:

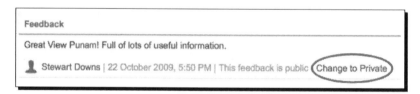

Punam clicks on the **Change to Private** button and to her delight sees that the feedback is now private:

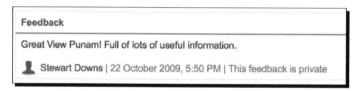

Feedback on your own View

Don't forget that you can give feedback on your own Views. This could be a good way of telling a group of people about your intentions behind creating the View without writing it into the content itself. It could also be used as a welcome message to a group of people who will be copying your View.

Best practice example – multi-page view

You have seen that each View you create in Mahara is essentially a single web page. On each of these web pages, you can show off a section of your ePortfolio or discuss a subject or topic. Imagine if you could link lots of these web pages together to make a website. You would then be able to create a more comprehensive story using each page to discuss a different topic.

In this section, we are going to show you a very simple way that you can use in order to link your Views together. We will be making our own menu bar as well as discussing the kind of things you might want to put into the different pages of your site.

For our case study, we will be using a multi-page view created by Derrin Kent, which you can see at `http://mahara.tdm.info/view/view.php?id=4`. Derrin had created a number of Views in his portfolio on topics that interested him, including WBL 2.0 (Work Based Learning), ePortfolios, ZPD (Zone of Proximal Development), Peak Oil, and Web 2.0. He realized that he wanted to link from his WBL 2.0 View to his other views because they were on related topics.

He decided that he would add a "related links" menu bar to all of these views so that it would be easy to navigate between them. This is just one idea about how you might like to use multi-page views, but here are a few more:

◆ In an artist's portfolio, you might want to have different Views to sort your work by media type (for example, animation, sculpture, 2D work) or into projects. You could then create a menu linking all of your work together from a home page. On the home page, you could describe a little about yourself and include some Profile Information so that people can get in touch with you. Then, all you need to do is send a link to your home page to others and they can view your entire portfolio.

◆ A teacher might want to create a series of Views on a particular subject. These could be organized by lesson so that each View is a different lesson with its own objectives and outcomes. All the Views can then be linked together so that the students can flick through them like a book.

◆ You might want to create some private Views that display all of your own reflective blogs rather than squashing them all into one View. Each View could contain a different Blog, for example, one may be personal, one may be related to a course you are taking, one may be on a subject that interests you, and so on. You can then link the Views together to have a quick way of seeing all of your blogs in one place. This would be great for reviewing and reflecting what you have been doing without having to go through each blog individually.

Now that you have a few ideas about the kind of multi-page View you might like to create, let's see how Derrin connected his "related topic" Views together.

Time for action – linking Views together to make a multi-page View

1. Insert a Text Box into one of the Views. Choose carefully where you would like this to be because it is going to contain the navigation for your site—either the top left or top right is a good place to choose.

2. Give your Text Box a relevant title (for example, Main Menu or Related Links) and in the body of the text enter the names of each View that you wish to link to. Put each name on a new line. Save the changes. Derrin called his menu **Related Links** and put it in the top left-hand side of his View. This is what it looks like on his View so far:

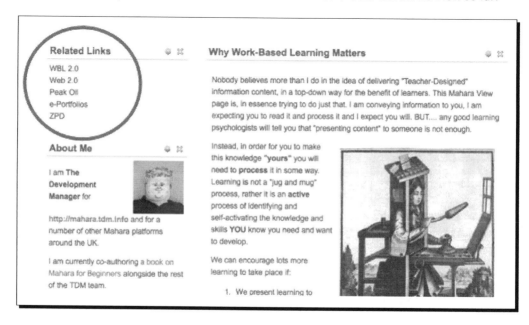

3. Now we need to link each line of text to the View it relates to. To do this, you will first need to visit the **My Views** section of **My Portfolio**. Find one of the other Views that you would like to link to and copy its URL (address link). You can do this by right-clicking on the title of the view and clicking on **Copy Link Location**. A more long-winded way of doing this is to open the View itself and to copy the address from the address bar.

4. Return to the initial View where you added the Text Box earlier. Select the relevant text and make a hyperlink to the address you just copied. Derrin is linking his Web 2.0 text to the View of the same name. Remember to give your link a relevant **Title** too:

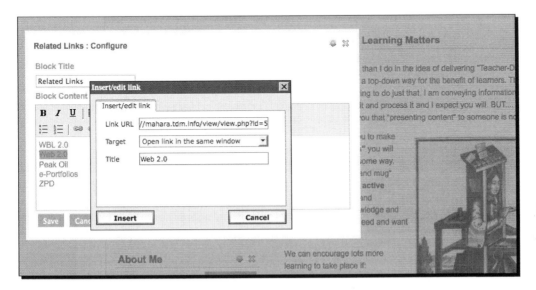

5. Do the same thing to create links to each of the other Views that will appear in your menu bar. To add a finishing touch, turn your links into a bulleted list:

Make copying links easier—use browser tabs

A lot of modern browsers now support a feature called **tabbing**. This means you can have more than one web page (or tab) open at the same time in the same browser window. You can use this feature to make it easier for you to copy the location of your Views to the Menu Text Box without having to keep switching windows. See `http://www.mozilla.com/en-US/firefox/tabs.html` for an introduction to tabbing in the Firefox web browser. Use *Ctrl+t* to open a new tab in most browsers (use *Apple* instead of *Ctrl* on a Mac).

6. You now have a Menu in one of your Views, but you probably want to replicate this so that each of the Views in the web page has its own Menu. To do this, copy the contents of the Text Box you just created.

7. In one of your other Views, create a new Text Box block. Position it in the same position on the View as the Menu you just made and give it the same title.

8. Paste the contents of the menu that you copied before, and click on **Save**. You will now have the same menu on a different View! Here is Derrin's menu on the **ZPD** View:

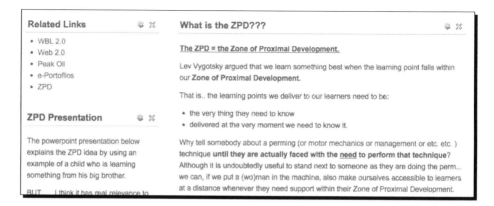

9. Repeat this for all the other Views that appear in the Menu. When you have finished, try clicking through to the different Views to test out your new "website".

What just happened?

You just saw how to link your Views together into a small website.

The links we created were simple HTML links. These links will take on the same style as the theme of Mahara, so their color and behavior (hover color) will be the same as for any other link you see on the site. One way to add a bit more detail to your link would be to change the color and format (embolden/underline/italics) using the text editor.

Assessing the quality of your View

So by now, you should have had plenty of practice setting up Views. We would like to encourage you to think about the quality of your View. The quality of your View is very important. If your View is to be available for others to see, then you want them to be enthused to read/watch/listen to what you have to say. If the View is just for personal reflection, you still want to be able to return to the View at a later date and still understand it, especially if you are going to use it in some kind of revision program.

We have devised a list of guidelines for you to assess your Views against. This list is grouped into two key sections that we believe are important in View quality: **Aesthetics** (layout, graphics, and so on) and **Content** (what you are adding, how relevant it is, and so on).

You may not agree with all of the guidelines, but hopefully it will help in providing a good basis from which you can assess the quality of your View. This checklist will be available for download from this book's demonstration Mahara site: `http://maharaforbeginners.tdm.info/`. In the downloadable version, we have provided simple checkboxes to the right of the criteria points for you to fill in if you wish to. Here is the checklist:

View quality checklist

The View quality checklist is divided into two sections, as follows:

Aesthetics

This section contains the following list:

◆ **A1**: Main body font is consistent throughout the View, apart from where changes are absolutely necessary (for example, to highlight a different point, or to leave a comment).

◆ **A2**: Main body font is relevant to the content. Use of serif/sans-serif fonts are appropriate.

◆ **A3**: Main body font isn't garish; it should be simple. Good fonts to use are: Serif—Garamond, Times, Baskerville, Century and Sans-serif—Helvetica, Verdana, Arial.

◆ **A4**: Heading text stands out from body text. It is either a different size of font or it is emboldened.

◆ **A5**: Heading font is consistent across the entire View.

◆ **A6**: There is an appropriate use of color. For example, a View to be shown to a younger audience may include bright, primary colors. A professional View may be toned down with only gray and black colors used. Hence, you can avoid using clashing colors.

◆ **A7**: Images in your View are of a sensible size. They don't dominate over other content by being too big.

◆ **A8**: Images are cut/cropped to the correct size before you upload them to your View. You don't have unnecessary detail in your images.

◆ **A9**: Images are of a good coloring. Your images don't look washed out or too bright.

◆ **A10**: Images are in a high resolution. Your images don't look pixelated or low quality.

◆ **A11**: The View is visually attractive. It includes a graphic of some kind. People looking at your View should want to read it.

◆ **A12**: There is an element of user initiative/creativity in the aesthetics of the View. This may include the creation of your own image, or an interesting color scheme.

◆ **A13**: Paragraphs are used appropriately.

◆ **A14**: Bullet pointed/numbered lists are used to break up long sections of text.

◆ **A15**: If you have developed a multi-page View, then the layout/design of each page is consistent. Each page doesn't use vastly different fonts/image styles.

◆ **A16**: The View doesn't appear too cluttered. There shouldn't be lots of text/images packed into one section of the View.

◆ **A17**: All space has been used effectively. There shouldn't be large spaces unless there absolutely must be.

◆ **A18**: Links in the View should stand out from the main body text.

◆ **A19**: All links should have the same color throughout the View.

◆ **A20**: All links should have the same style throughout the View.

Content

This section contains the following list:

◆ **C1**: The content isn't simply a repetition of fact. The View contains personal responses to the content. Arguments/opinions are included.

◆ **C2**: The thoughts are well structured and original.

◆ **C3**: The View has a clear purpose/objective. It should be there for a reason.

◆ **C4**: Linked to point C3, an introductory sentence or paragraph should be included to communicate the key objective of the View.

◆ **C5**: The content is free of grammatical/punctuation errors.

◆ **C6**: Colloquialism/slang is used only when appropriate to the subject of the View or to your style of reflection.

◆ **C7**: Video included should be short, succinct, and add value to the View content. As a guide, videos longer than two minutes should be considered before inclusion. Videos of 30 seconds are ideal.

◆ **C8**: Audio should also add value to the content and be of a high quality. Audio hasn't just been included "for the sake of it".

◆ **C9**: Your media content doesn't distract from the main body of writing.

- ◆ **C10**: Content is interesting. Even if what you are writing about isn't to the readers' normal interest, they should be hooked by a well presented, convincing, structured View. Dry content (for example, mathematical equations) has been padded out with interesting quotations/historical references/practical video examples relating to the subject.

- ◆ **C11**: Any arguments you make are polite and respectful. You show sensitivity to different audiences and do not offend them by your writing.

- ◆ **C12**: None of your content is repetitive. You haven't duplicated images or ideas.

- ◆ **C13**: Wherever relevant, you have summarized your content with an indication of what has been learned.

- ◆ **C14**: Your content shows research on the subject being discussed. A certain amount of work required prior to View creation is evident.

- ◆ **C15**: In the case of multi-linked Views, there is a logical order to the pages. Each tells a separate section of the whole story.

- ◆ **C16**: All links in your content are 'live'. None of them link to dead pages or pages that have altered from the original intended content.

- ◆ **C17**: Linked-to content is of a high quality. Content in external websites is relevant to the original subject.

- ◆ **C18**: Links are well-labeled. They give a clear indication of what content you should expect to see when you click on them.

- ◆ **C19**: You have summarized your content with an indication of what has been learned.

Have a go hero – make a top quality View

You have learned all there is to know about making your own View in Mahara and seen two case studies: one View on the Tudors by Punam and a multi-page View by Derrin. Use this information, and the View Quality Guide we have just discussed to make a View on the demonstration site `http://maharaforbeginners.tdm.info`. Your View could be on anything you want—sport, politics, hobbies, art, music, film, and so on.

You should make your View in the group called **Mahara: Best Practice**. We have chosen the best examples from the selection of Views that are created to be displayed on the home page of the site. We don't mind what topic you choose; we want to see you coming up with ideas for making your Views interesting, innovative, and of good quality. The examples we have used in this chapter are also in that group to help you get you started.

Summary

In this chapter, we learned a lot about Views. You saw how you can make a new View from scratch and edit it to contain the kind of content that you want to add. You also saw how to control who sees your View as well as when they see it. We saw how to go back and edit your View once you have created it. Also, you copied someone else's View into your portfolio area. You had an introduction to the View feedback system in Mahara and placed your first feedback on the View, deciding whether or not you wanted to make it public. Finally, you saw an example of good View practice and we encouraged you to think about the content of your View by providing you with some View Quality Guidelines.

Now that you've learned about your Profile, Files, Blogs, and Views, you're ready to learn all about the social networking facilities in Mahara. We started to discuss social networking in this chapter when we mentioned Groups and Friends. That is the topic of the next chapter.

5
Working in Groups and Interacting with Friends

By now, you must have added your "stuff" to Mahara and discovered how to organize it into web pages using views. In this chapter, we will find out how we can connect with other Mahara users using groups and friends. This is where Mahara really comes to life, with people being able to discuss topics of common interest in forums and share views with each other. So what are we waiting for? Let's get social!

In this chapter, we shall:

- ◆ Learn how to make our own groups
- ◆ See what we can do in a group
- ◆ Create and participate in forums
- ◆ Learn how to find and join other groups
- ◆ Start building our network of friends

Groups

Groups in Mahara are a way of bringing users together into places where they can collaborate and share ideas. Groups may be created for different numbers of users. Commonly, you might create a group based around a common interest area or hobby. For example, if you are interested in playing guitar, you might create a group called "Guitar Playing Techniques". Groups may also be based around a course in which all learners of the course are members of the group.

You can give your group a name and description, and decide who can enter the group. Here is what you can do in a Mahara Group:

1. **Configure discussion forums**: This is where all the group members can discuss issues related to key topics in the group.

2. **Create group views**: Here, users can view group views and, can also collaborate to create new group views.

3. **Share group files**: You can allow members of the group to upload their own files to share with other group members.

----- **Janet Norman form PI-Inc thinks** -----

This is really where Mahara gets very interesting for me. I want my users to be communicating in common interest groups that relate to the type of research and development they are involved in. We want to use Mahara for improving communication between staff members in other roles as well. Communities of practice can form where marketing experts share their ideas and techniques by sharing views that they have created. Managers can use forums to discuss practical applications of procedures and compare experiences, giving advice wherever they feel they can. Strategists can work collaboratively on tenders. In different ways, Mahara groups can offer PI Inc people a real digital place where we can share innovative ideas and chat to each other about questions and problems that we may be facing.

Let's get started by showing you how to set up your first group.

Time for action – creating a group

Let's first learn how to create a Mahara group:

1. Click on the **Groups** option in the menu bar. This is the area containing all the options that you need to access the social aspects of Mahara.

2. By default, you are now on the **My Groups** page. Currently, you don't belong to any groups, but that's about to change. Click on the **Create Group** button as shown in the following screenshot:

3. You will now see the **Create Group** page. This contains all the options you need to configure your new group. Start by giving your group a relevant name in the **Group name** box.

4. Next, take some time to fill in the **Group Description**. The information that you enter here will show up in the group "About" page.

5. The **Group Type** option allows you to decide how other users join your group. There are three possible types of groups available to normal Mahara users. Administrators and Staff Members have three additional group types, which we will introduce to you in Chapter 7. Don't worry about them for now. Just select the **Open Membership Standard** group option.

6. That's all, there is to it! Click on **Save Group** to finish.

What just happened?

We just saw how to make a new Mahara group.

Revisit the **My Groups** page. Here you will see the group that you have just created along with the title and description you had entered earlier. It is important that you choose a sensible summary for your group so that when you are looking through all your groups on this page later, you will know exactly what the different groups are for. You will notice that the **My Groups** page also shows a snapshot of all the members that currently belong to the group:

Clinical Trials   Edit

Janet Norman,   Delete

Medicinal technology can be used to aid the treatment of a wide variety of illnesses. Use this gr...

Members: Janet Norman, Sally Brock, John Reeves,

Finally, this is the place you should come to if you want to edit or delete the group. The **Edit** option allows you to change any of the group settings you originally chose. Clicking on the **Delete** option brings up a warning page asking if you would like to delete the group as shown below:

Always be certain that you know you are doing the right thing before you decide to delete your group. There may be important forums or views in there that other users want to keep.

Now, before we go on to explore what else we can do in our group, let's have a look at the different group types available to us.

Group types

In the last *Time for action*, we discovered that when we create a new group we can decide what type it is going to be. There are three types of 'Standard' Groups that normal Mahara users can choose between:

- **Open membership**: Any logged in user of the site can join your group.
- **Request membership**: Users of the site can decide to request membership to your group. You then have the option of whether or not to accept them.
- **Invite only**: Only site users to whom you have sent an invitation are able to join your group. These users can decide whether or not to accept or decline your invitation.

In order to get a better idea about how these different group types affect how people join our group, let's discuss each type in more detail and think up a few scenarios where they might be used.

Open membership groups

When you choose to create an open membership group, you are opening up your community to participation by all registered site users. In making this decision, you are saying that you don't mind who joins your group and, in fact, that you want to encourage participation by as many users as possible. You are also giving your users the freedom to leave the group at any time. This group type is great for a community space where you want to encourage a large number of people to join in and participate in the open discussion. Many of the groups on the `www.mahara.org` website, for example, are open membership groups. Why restrict community interaction unless you really need to?

----- **Neil from Training 4 Work thinks** -----

*I would like to set up a social area for my learners called "Sports".
I want everyone to be able to participate without any restrictions on
joining. I want joining up to be as simple as clicking on a Join button
for the group. Open membership seems to be the option I should
go for.*

Request membership groups

This is where you start getting more protective of your group. You aren't opening up
the group to all users, but getting users to send a **Request**—asking for your permission
before they can join in. This is a good way of restricting group access to users who have
an active interest in joining you. When users request to join your group, they can give a
short description explaining why. You should think carefully before creating this group type
because it means, potentially, that you will have to monitor and respond to lots of requests
to join.

----- **Janet Norman form PI-Inc thinks** -----

*I'm really excited thinking about all the different groups I can make.
One idea I have is to have a company-wide PI Inc policy discussion
group. I want the members of the group to actively engage in the
discussions. I think the request membership group would be ideal
for this because they can give a short message explaining why they
would like to join.*

Invite only groups

This is the most restricted group type. The group creator has full control over who they want
in the group. This group type is useful when you know exactly who you want in your group. A
good example would be a scenario where you only want people in an existing focus group to
become members of your Mahara group. In this scenario, you could just invite the members
of the focus group to join. They, of course, have the right to turn either accept or turn down
your invitation.

----- **Neil from Training 4 Work thinks** -----

Our finance department would like to discuss company finance reports. I want to choose exactly a group who joins it, and so, I'm going to choose the invite-only group type.

In Mahara there are other group types, which are available to Administrators and Staff Members only. There are two types of **Course Groups** and another standard group type known as a **Controlled Membership** group. These group types allow you to get learners submitting work to you for formal assessment. The controlled membership group also allow you to dictate exactly who is/isn't a member of your group. Neil has these higher-level powers within his Mahara site and has indicated that he is interested in using Course groups. See Chapter 7 if you think this is what you want to do.

Now let's see what we can do in our new group.

Navigating your new group

Before we start looking at group members, forums, views, and files, let's get used to navigating around our group and take a look at the **About** page.

Time for action – opening up and navigating around your group

Let's navigate around the group we want:

1. In the **My Groups** section, open up the group you would like to navigate around by clicking on its name. In the following example, we click on the **Clinical Trials** group we created for Janet:

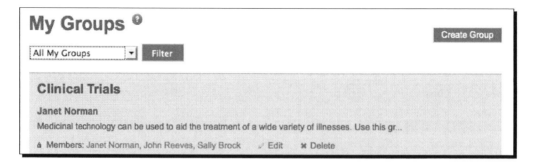

2. You will now see all the options available for your group in a menu bar. The tabs are **About**, **Members**, **Forums**, **Views**, and **Files**. Try clicking on each of these to get used to navigating around your group.

3. Return to the default group page by clicking the **About** tab.

4. The **About** page gives an overview of the group. Including a description of what the group is about, who administers and moderates it (we will see who these people are later), when it was created, how many members' files and folders there are, and the latest forum posts. You can also edit or delete the group from the **About** page. You can use the Mahara Text Editor that you used in Chapter 2 to add images, video clips, hyperlinks, or decorative text as you wish. Here is the screenshot of the concise and simple **About** page that Janet has created for the **Clinical Trials** group:

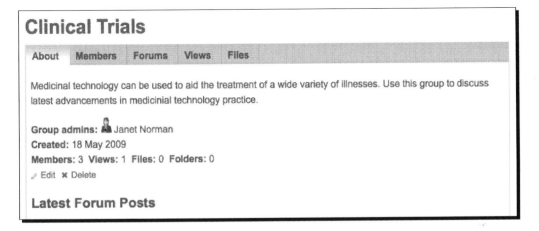

5. And that's all there is to navigating your group!

What just happened?

You just had a brief introduction to what a group looks like and how to navigate it using the group tabs. We also had a look at the group **About** page and how we can use it to see an overview of what's going on in our group.

There is another quick way to navigate your group, which we will quickly look at now.

The groups shortcut sideblock

Whenever you do anything with group, a handy little feature of Mahara is the groups shortcut sideblock. It will usually be on the right-hand side of your screen and look a little like the following screenshot of the **Clinical Trials** group:

Clinical Trials

- About
- Members
- Forums
    - Ethical and Legal Issues
- Views
- Files

This list is a great way for quickly navigating to different options for your group. It also gives you a snapshot of what's going on in the group by showing you which forums exist.

Have a go hero – set up some new groups and create their About pages

It is time to set up some of your own groups. If you don't yet have your own Mahara site, feel free to register yourself at either: http://maharaforbeginners.tdm.info or http://demo.mahara.org. Both of these sites offer safe havens where you can experiment with group creation at will.

If you already have a Mahara site, you must be wise enough to put in a bit of advance thinking before you start clicking on the Mahara buttons. Why not brainstorm a list of groups that you would like to set up onto a sheet of paper first? You can then start deciding what group type you think you should choose for each of your new groups. When you are ready, go ahead and start setting up your different groups in the Mahara space. As you set up each and every group, put a little bit of thought and love into your **About** page. It is, after all, the first introduction your new group members will get to your group.

As we said, you can put anything on this **About** page, including images, embedded videos from YouTube or hyperlinks to an associated Moodle course (for example) or to another relevant website.

Joining an open membership group

By now, you should have an empty group set up with the relevant settings. But a group is nothing without its community members!

Let's see how a user would join an open membership group.

Time for action – joining a group in maharaforbeginners.tdm.info

Let's see how easy it is to join a Mahara group:

1. Log in to `http://maharaforbeginners.tdm.info` with your username and password.

2. Click on **Groups** in the main menu bar.

3. Click on the **Find Groups** sub-menu tab.

4. You will see all the groups that are available to you in `http://maharaforbeginners.tdm.info`. Browse through the groups until you find one called **ePortfolios: Best Practice**. Remember, you can always use the query box to search for any group you want if you already know its name.

5. When you have found this group, you will see that you have an option to **Join this group**. This button is present on all open membership groups. Click on **Join this group**:

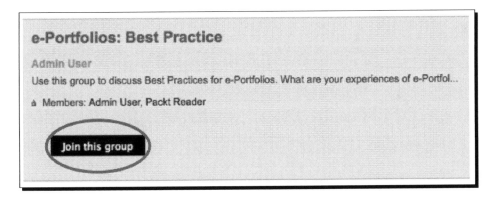

6. That's all there is to it. You have just joined your first Mahara group. You will get a little message telling you that **You are now a group member**.

What just happened?

You just joined a group in `http://maharaforbeginners.tdm.info`. We think it would be great if readers of this book could use the groups and discussion area in this site to give feedback on things that they have read in the book or generally to discuss Mahara and ePortfolios.

Have a look around the other groups in the site and see if there are any that grab your interest. Why not join up to some more groups—or even set up some new groups of your own? When you are bored of practicing in this environment, you should move over to spend most of your time at the international community site: `http://mahara.org`. Here you will find a vibrant international community of Mahara users—all of them working together to improve the Mahara experience for everyone.

Managing your group members

If, when you made your group earlier, you made an open membership group, then it is possible that people have already started joining you. If you chose a request membership or invite-only group, then you won't have many members as of yet. We will see later in the chapter how to **Invite** members and respond to other users' **Join** requests.

Janet Norman can now see that new users have started to join her group. She would like to know how she can view more details about who is in her group as well as how to manage them.

When we talk about "managing members", we mean the ability to decide who stays in your group and to determine what roles users in the group have assigned to them.

Time for action – removing group members and changing roles

So, let's get going and find out how to manage our group members:

1. Start by clicking on the **Members** tab of the **Groups** menu bar.

2. You will now see a screen with all your group members listed. In Janet's Clinical Trials group there are currently three members indicated by the info text at the bottom of the page. These members are displayed in a box similar to the following:

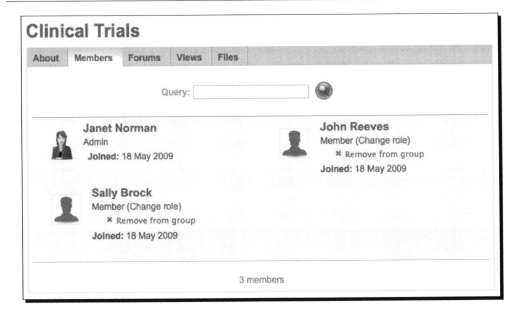

3. When your group starts growing it will be more difficult to find your users. You can use the **Query** search box to find the user you are looking for. Type the name of the person you would like to search for in your group. Janet Norman has said that she would like John Reeves to become a group administrator. To show querying in action, lets type "John" in the query box:

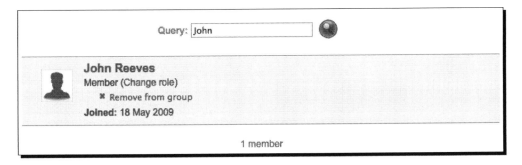

4. Now we want to change the role for John. To do this, start by clicking the **Change role** option:

5. Next you will see a screen inviting you to switch the role of the user. Switch your group member to have an administrator role by selecting **Admin** from the drop-down list. To complete the action, click **Submit**:

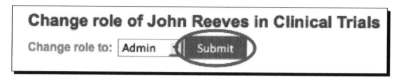

6. Finally, you may want to completely remove a user from your group. To do so, click on the **Remove from group** button next to the user's name. You must be sure before you do this because the user will be instantly removed, if you make a mistake you will have to add them again from scratch:

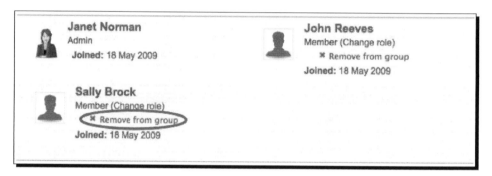

What just happened?

We just learned how we can manage our group users as a Group Administrator.

We saw in the last *Time for action* that you are able to assign roles to your users (that is, whether to make them a Group Administrator or not). Let's have a look at what is the difference between a Group Administrator and a Group Member:

- ◆ **Group Administrator:** A Group Administrator can do anything in a group, including managing users, editing the group settings, creating forums, editing forum posts, creating views, and uploading files. The person who creates a group is automatically a Group Administrator.

- ◆ **Group Member:** A member can create forum topics, group views, and upload group files. Members are simply users in your group who aren't administrators.

You should think carefully about who you want to administer your group. Adding new administrators helps to ease the pressure on you for updating and monitoring your group because you can share the load with another member of staff. On the other hand, you must be sure that your group administrators know what they are doing, otherwise they could do something damaging such as deleting a forum or accidentally removing users. To prevent that, they should probably be handed this chapter to read first!

Our group now has some members, so it's time to start getting them talking and interacting within your Group Forums.

Pop quiz – creating Mahara groups

1. Who is allowed to join an open membership group?
2. What does it mean to make your group publicly viewable?
3. What can a Group Administrator do that a Group Member can't?

Group forums

The Cambridge Online Dictionary (`http://dictionary.cambridge.org`) defines a forum as *a situation or meeting in which people can talk about a problem or matter*. Traditionally, a forum used to be a physical place where people could join together and share ideas (think of the Romans). Nowadays, thanks to internet technology, people don't even need to be on the same continent to discuss things in this way!

Forums are one of the most important features we will use for socializing. Group members are able to talk about a topic in forums and can comment on each other's ideas or suggestions.

Mahara groups give you the ability to add forums at will, allowing your group members to discuss any issues they would like to. Each forum can have lots of users in it—all of them making posts. Posts are simply text comments, and they can be used to ask questions or to respond to elements of a discussion. Each group can have more than one forum, each with a different topic.

Let's go back to Janet and see what ideas she has about how she can use forums in her Clinical Trials group.

----- **Janet Norman form PI-Inc thinks** -----

We know how important it is for our clinical trials to be conducted in a legal and moral way. To help with this, it would be great to get a legal and ethical discussion forum going where our experts can talk about the latest legislation and ethical issues that are relevant to the way we conduct our clinical trials.

The forum Janet has suggested is great for gathering information from different users in one place.

Here is what Neil from Training 4 Work thinks about forums:

----- **Neil from Training 4 Work thinks** -----

We are coming to the end of a program for some of our learners. It would be great if we could get a discussion going on the users' experience of using Mahara for reflective learning. A course experience forum in the course group would be perfect for this so that the users can let us know what they think of the online and offline elements of our training program, and suggest what improvements we can make next time we run it.

Hopefully you will now have some idea now about the different kinds of forum you may want to have in your own group.

Time for action – creating a forum

Now, let's go ahead and see how we set up the legal forum for Janet:

1. From the group homepage, click on the **Forums** tab.

2. You will probably see that there are currently no forums in your group. Let's quickly change that by clicking on the **New Forum** button.

3. The add forum page is now open. Give your forum a relevant **Title**.

4. Then fill in the **Description** giving a simple explanation of what the forum will be used for.

5. You will also see a little button that says **Settings**; click it. There is an option to automatically subscribe users; if this is set to **Yes** then all group members will start receiving e-mail updates about this forum. Janet wants her users to decide for themselves if they would like to subscribe so we leave it set to **No**.

6. There is also an option to add Moderators for the forum. Moderators are non-admin members who you have confidence in to edit and delete other peoples' topics or posts. Janet has decided that she would like to have one Moderator called Sally Brock who is the head of the Clinical Trials steering group. To make someone a Moderator, simply click on their name under the **Potential Moderators** section (1) and click the right arrow (2). You will now see them listed under Current Moderators (3):

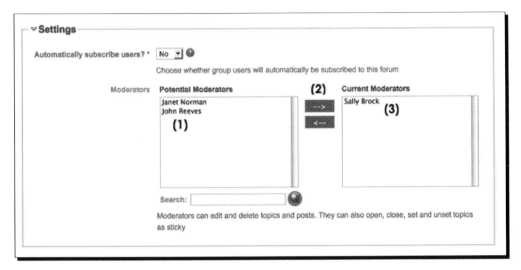

7. Finally, click on the **Save** button to finish. You will see a screen similar to this showing your newly created forum:

What just happened?

You just saw how easy it is to create your first group forum.

The Mahara forums are as good as any you will find on the Internet—so take advantage of the feature. Think about discussions you have at the moment that require meeting up in a physical location and consider making an online Mahara forum for them so that you can chat at distance. Why spend hours talking in face-to-face meetings? You could get all the serious discussions done before you turn up to a meeting, cutting down meeting time to focus on making the decisions. Use the online forums to debate issues first, and then meet face-to-face to make the decisions.

The other great thing about Mahara forums is that they can serve as a permanent online record of thought. Often, people tend to "craft" their thinking more carefully when they put their thoughts into writing than they do when they are speaking aloud. Users can go back time and again to revisit carefully-crafted comments that were made a long time ago, which may still be useful today.

With group forums, you are able to keep the discussions in relevant and controlled areas. You can fully decide who does and doesn't see the forum and who you would like to administer or moderate it.

We also introduced the concept of a forum moderator. Let's have a look at this in more detail.

Forum moderation

It may be important that your group forums are moderated. In a Mahara group a forum can be edited by Group Administrators and Forum Moderators.

By forum moderation, we mean the allocation a few special people to actively "make the discussions happen". A moderator will generally "conduct" the following phases of a forum:

1. Clearly present the topic up for discussion.
2. Engage participants.
3. Manage the discussion process: linking the thought threads, widening out the topic, engaging responses from the more passive, and so on.
4. "Ending" the discussion when appropriate: perhaps with personalized feedback to some of the participants and a generic discussion "summary" or "conclusion" for the benefit of all.

Not all forums have to follow the framework suggested above, of course. Many forums are more open-ended in nature and many can be much more "passively" moderated.

Another responsibility of a forum moderator is to ensure that people are 'behaving themselves'. What exactly we mean by behaving yourself is entirely up to us. Typically, a forum moderator should establish a set of ground rules for what is and isn't acceptable behavior. Common rules might include the exclusion of abusive language, or a negative attitude to other people's postings.

Once the ground rules are established, it is a good idea for a moderator to make these clear and available to forum members. Perhaps they could include a link to the code of conduct in the forum description. This way the users will know the ground rules before they even start posting.

It is a good idea to replicate forum moderation standards across the entire Mahara site. Your Mahara Site Administrator may even have set up a code of practice for Forum contribution as an element on your site's Terms and Conditions page. The important point is that you should be seeking to develop community standards from the onset, which become the culture for how people behave.

These extracts from a classic article called Netiquette by Gary Alexander get you thinking about how people should expect to behave in forum settings (`http://sustainability. open.ac.uk/gary/netique.htm`).

Moderators should also try to be active in discussions. Here are a few things you could do as a moderator:

- Encourage users to send requests to you for how the forum should operate.
- Reply to threads, giving useful information.
- Take time to listen to people, giving praise to good postings or topics with useful information.
- Be diplomatic with users who aren't following guidelines. Message them privately, not publicly. Usually a polite request to tone down their behavior will do the job.
- Be the most obsessive user of the forum. Be interested in the discussion. Spark discussion yourself.

On the forum page you will see there are a few options for managing our new forum. We will briefly discuss these now.

Managing your forum

You may want to edit your forum after some time. To do this, simply use the **Edit forum** option. You will see all the same options that you were presented when you created the forum.

You may also want to delete the forum. Perhaps, you realize that nobody is engaging in discussion with that particular forum and it doesn't matter even if you delete it because there aren't many topics. To do this, click the **Delete forum** button. You will get a message prompting you to confirm the action.

Be careful when deleting forums

When you delete a forum, all of the content will be removed, including topics, posts, and moderators. You really need to be sure before you delete any forums in Mahara because they could contain valuable information.

Finally, one superb feature of forums is the ability to subscribe to them. Subscription is just like subscribing to a weekly magazine. Instead of receiving mail through your front door, you will get live Mahara notifications giving you details of new forums posts that are added. Click **Subscribe to forum** to do this:

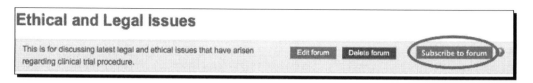

If you want to stop receiving notifications of forum posts, click **Unsubscribe from forum**:

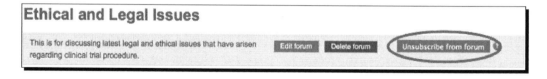

The exciting bit: Forum topics

Now that we have our forum in place, it's time to start adding the questions and comments that will make it into a lively social discussion area. To do this, we first need to start using topics.

Topics are issues (or topics) that people want to discuss. A forum that works, remember, will usually be one where the group members have an extrinsic necessity (for example, part of their job role) or an intrinsic desire to engage with it (useful information to gain, important decisions to be made, fun and laughter to be had).

Forum discussion frameworks

A forum can be made up of many different topics with wide ranging issues. The best discussions frameworks are those that lead to some sort of "outcome" or conclusion. Some generically useful discussion frameworks include:

◆ **Comparing**: For example, "What are the similarities and differences between food we eat today and food they ate in Tudor England?"

◆ **Detecting differences**: For example, "What different reactions are there to our company's marketing campaigns in different countries?"

◆ **Putting in order**: For example, "Put the list of ten course topics in order of one to ten. Number one was the most interesting and number ten was the least interesting. Then tell us why you felt like this."

◆ **Choosing Candidates**: For example, "Which three course books does our community feel we should recommend to all new students on our next course? Tell us why you chose these particular three." (One of the most famous Choosing Candidates discussions is the "Hot Air Balloon debate" in which participants have to decide who gets thrown overboard from an air balloon which is falling fast towards the ground (the sandbags, of course, have long gone overboard!)

◆ **Question and Answer**: For example, many of the practical support forums on `http://mahara.org`

◆ **Ideas from a central theme**: For example, "Let's discuss new research approaches." This then gets broken down into sub-discussions as to the relevant merits of the individual approaches.

◆ **Implications and Interpretations**: For example, "What would life have been like when people didn't have the advanced medical facilities we have today? " or "How do you think Henry VIIIth would have practically coped or suffered with the gangrene in his leg?"

◆ **Surveys of Opinion**: For example, "Tell us three things you think we should do differently in our course next year."

◆ **Planning Projects**: For example, 1. Brainstorm ideas, 2. Prioritize actions, 3. Allocate responsibilities, 4. Report back on progress, 5. Celebrate successes.

◆ **Combining Versions**: For example, "Let's read all the views that individual users have submitted to our group and then identify which are the most important elements we think we should include in a common group view on this topic."

◆ **Layout problems**: For example, "Let's discuss how we lay out our group view." or "How shall we set up our open plan office?"

This is not an exhaustive list, of course. The most important thing is to try to set up discussions with a clear sense of purpose or "outcome" to the debate. You do this because you need to give your forum participants a reason to post.

Don't get us wrong, depending upon the engagement and motivation of the group a generic forum title such as:

- "Talk about Dogs"

  Could, in fact, generate just as much discussion as a "choosing candidates" discussion like:

- "The queen of England likes Corgis and Winston Churchill should have had a bulldog. Say which breed of dog you think is best suited to (Queen Elizabeth I or for example the CEO of PI Inc) and tells us why you chose this breed."

  Or a "comparing" discussion such as:

- "Cats make better pets than dogs. Discuss."

There is nothing to say that you have to use Mahara forums to set up "outcomes-oriented" discussion frameworks, we are simply putting this idea forward for you as food for thought.

Let's go back to Janet and see what kinds of topics she thinks could be included in her legal and ethical forum for the Clinical Trials group.

----- Janet Norman form PI-Inc thinks -----

One of my colleagues said that they would like a place where they can discuss if withholding medicine in clinical trials is ethical. There are implications and interpretations to be discussed here so I instantly suggested that we set this up as a topic in the Clinical Trials group's Legal and Ethical Forum.

Time for action – adding a discussion topic

So let's make our first forum topic:

1. Start by re-opening the forum you created earlier. To do this, we click on the **Forum** tab of the clinical trials group. You will see all the forums that exist in this group. Click on the name of the forum you would like to add a topic to. For our example, we click on the **Clinical Trials** forum.

2. You will then see a screen listing all the options for managing your forum that we discussed earlier. Simply click on **New Topic** to start making the topic.

3. Use the next screen to add a **Subject** and **Body**. The subject should be descriptive of exactly what you will be talking about in this topic. The body information should contain some more information about what it is you want to discuss, perhaps giving examples or posing questions to other users. You may want to set up an 'outcomes-oriented' discussion framework in your description to stimulate conversation. The screen will look like the following:

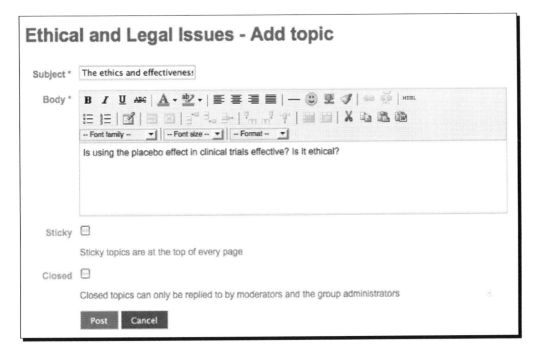

4. There are two other options on this page to make the topic **Sticky** or **Closed**. These options are only available to a Group Administrator or Forum Moderator. We are going to leave these set to the default option of unchecked.

5. When you are happy with your topic, click **Post** to add it to the forum, otherwise, click **Cancel**. And there you go, you have added you first forum post!

What just happened?

You just saw how easy it is to create your first forum topic. You gave it a relevant name and description and posted it to the forum. Now all you have to do is wait for people to start responding to you so that you can develop the discussion.

Let's take a brief look at how adding this post has affected the options available to us in the forum. For this example, we navigate back to the Ethical and Legal Issues forum. We can now see the topic we just created and its description as well as who has posted. As an Administrator you have the option to delete or edit the topic. Normal members do not have this option.

There is also the ability to quickly apply 'actions' to any topic. To do this, check the checkbox to the left of the topic box (1). Then use the down arrow at the top and bottom of the page to apply new options to a topic (2). When you have chosen an action, click **Update selected topics** (3). This is a good way of applying changes such as making topics sticky to more than one topic in your forum:

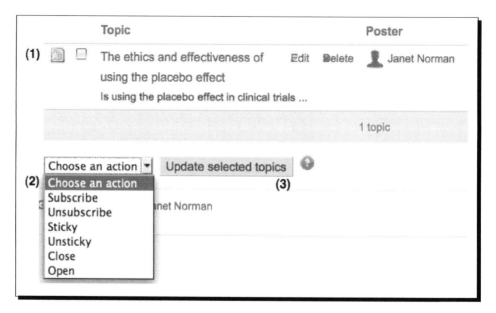

We also saw in the last *Time for action* that Group Administrators and Forum Moderators have two extra options when they are making a new topic. These are to make a topic **Sticky** or **Closed**:

- **Sticky topic:** Choose this option if you have lots of forum topics, and you would like this particular one to stand out from the rest by staying 'glued' to the top of the forum.

- **Closed topic:** These topics can only be replied to by Forum Moderators and Administrators for the group. Use these topics if you don't want other users to comment.

Sticky topics are really useful. Imagine that your forum is now really popular with lots of good advice going into the various posts and topics. This is when it becomes likely that topics start getting replicated and people begin discussing issues that have already been discussed. A good idea would be to create a sticky topic that stays at the top of the forum and brings together all the topics that are commonly discussed in the forum, linking the user to the correct area of discussion. This means that the user won't have to spend a long time searching through all the forums to find the answer they are looking for.

Such a topic could also be made closed. You wouldn't want this topic to be added to by general group users. It could be organized and managed by the group Moderator.

Naming forums and their topic subjects

Now that we've just created our first forum, let's think a little bit about how we want to name our forums and topics. Each forum in your group should be given a sufficiently general name with the idea being that it will be made up of a number of different topic threads that are all related to it. While the forum titles should be sufficiently general, the topic titles should all be specific and describe exactly what it is that will be spoken about.

For example, one Mahara site may have a group called "Olympics". A good forum title would be "Track and Field" because it is general and covers a wide topic. Then the "Track and Field" forum could have titles such as "Not enough funding for UK athletics" or "Which country is the best at track and field?" The topic subjects are more specific and targeted.

Posting to a topic

So we know how to make a new forum topic and how to administer forums, but what if we have found something in the forum that interests us and we want to respond to it? This is where posts come into the picture. You can have any number of posts for a topic in your forum.

Janet Norman has let me know that she has seen that a member of the site has added a response to the topic I helped her to create. She would really like to reply but doesn't know how to.

Time for action – replying to a topic post

So let's find how to reply to the posts:

1. Find and open the topic you want to reply to. You can do this by clicking a "recent forum posts" link in your group **About** page. More commonly though you would click the **Forum** tab in the group.

2. Then click on the link to the forum that contains the topic you want to reply to. Janet clicks into her ethical and legal issues forum:

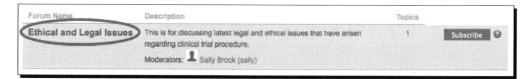

3. You will now see the topics listed in the forum. Click into the topic that you want to add a response to. Janet clicks into her ethics and placebo effect topic:

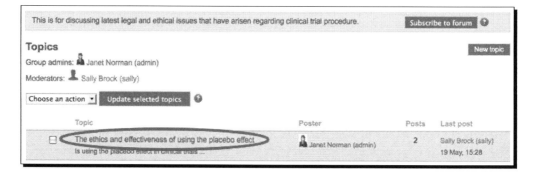

4. For each topic post, you will see that there are options to the bottom-right to **Reply**, **Edit**, or **Delete**. You will only see all three options if you are a forum administrator or moderator. A standard group user will just have the ability to reply. Click on **Reply** to make your response to the post:

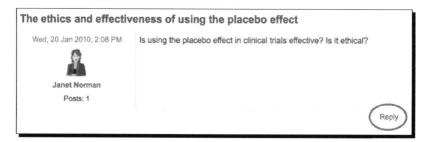

5. You will then see an editor that you can use to enter your response. Optionally you can also click to add a new title but often you will want the title to stay the same as the original topic. When you are happy with your response, click **Post**.

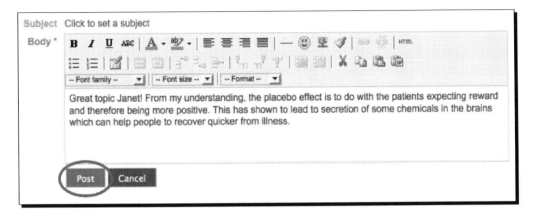

6. That's it! You now know everything you need to get actively involved in Mahara forum discussions. You should now see your response displayed below the original:

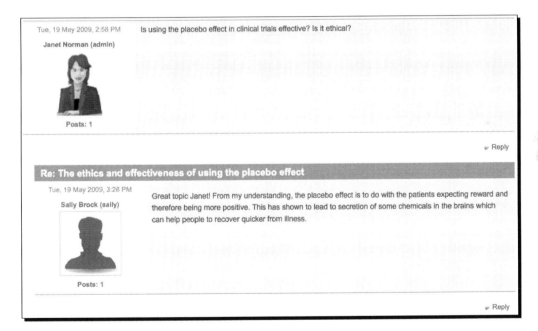

What just happened?

We have now covered all there is to know about Mahara group forums. You have created some forums in your site and seen how to start discussion topics as well as how to respond to other users' posts.

One thing to note about posting to forums is that you can edit any posts that you create, so you don't have to worry about making sure they are perfect the first time.

Pop quiz – group Forums

1. What is the job of a forum Moderator? What can they do?

2. What is a sticky forum topic? When might you use one?

3. What is a good system for naming your forums and topics?

We will now move on to looking at the other shared features of a group: files and views.

Group files

In your group you can also add "stuff" to share with everyone. The files you add to the group can then be used in group views or downloaded by the other group members. The group's file area works in exactly the same way as uploading your own file. Click on the **Files** tab in the group menu bar and have a go at uploading a file into the group.

Those who have an eagle eye will notice that there is a slight difference in the options for uploading a file to a group. You are given options for deciding what the permissions are for the file:

By default both **Admin** and **Member** are able to **View**, **Edit**, and **Publish** the file. If you want, you could decide to reduce the permissions to just allow group admins to see a file you upload; the choice is yours. This facility could come in very handy if you want to include progress reporting spreadsheets that only the tutors (but not the learners) get to see, for example.

If we set this possibility of fine-tuning access and permissions to one side, though, the great thing to notice about group files is that everyone in the group can access, edit, and publish any of them if you allow them to. This facility becomes even more useful when we think that we are able to link to these files from within Mahara group views and that is the topic of the next section.

Group views

The next feature of a group that will be useful for you is the group views option. Click on the Views tab to navigate here. The views section for your group will currently be empty and looks a little like the following screenshot:

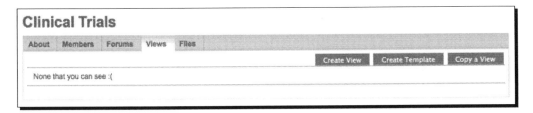

You have learned all about Mahara views in Chapters 2 and 4, so we won't repeat that here. Instead we will find out what is different about a group view and start thinking about how we can use them to improve our communication and to share information.

A group view is simply a normal view that can be seen by all members of the group. When you are creating a group view, you will notice that you don't have access to all the same blocks that you did when making your own views. You can't add any of your own profile information or blogs to a group view. The only blocks that you are able to add to a group view are:

♦ **External Feed**: RSS Feeds

♦ **Files, images and videos**: External Video, Group Files, Group Folders, HTML, An Image, Embedded Media

♦ **General**: Text box

So why would we want to create a group view? Group views are great for sharing ideas collaboratively. Different users can work together to edit a web page. It is a great way of keeping common information sheets, which could contain instructions or ideas. The ability of views to pull in image and video media from external sources will enable you to quickly show your group a host of rich interactive content without sending them a list of links. Let's hear what ideas Punam, Neil, and Janet have for how they can use group views:

----- Punam from Pennytown Primary thinks -----

Group views will be excellent for me because I can effectively create interactive online worksheets that are organized into specific areas of my site. I can share a worksheet view that I have just created about rivers in a geography group. I can use a text box in the view to get learners entering factual information they can discover about named rivers (length in kilometers, geographic location, and so on). I can also encourage the children to collaborate further by adding more blocks to this group view: getting them each to add their own artwork and web links in order to make an online collage that they can go home and show their parents online.

----- Janet Norman form PI-Inc thinks -----

Group views will be useful for us to work together in our Clinical Trials group to produce a document showing and summarizing key action points that have arisen in our group discussions. This will be helpful to steer company thinking in respect to the current situation with our clinical trial procedures. The view we create could be used as a reference document in any strategic meetings that we have in the future.

----- Neil from Training 4 Work thinks -----

I am going to set up a group view for electrical engineering topics-of-the-day related to information I read in monthly magazines. This will go into our electrical engineering group. Users of the group can then all access the view for up-to-date information about electrical engineering. This will be completely separate from our formal accreditation process, as it will be more of an informal interest group.

Finding Groups

We have covered everything there is to know about the features of a Mahara group, let's start thinking about joining other groups. Now, it's all good and well having groups in your Mahara, but what happens when it starts to get overloaded with not just tens, but potentially hundreds of them? How will I find not only my own groups but groups that I don't own? The answer to this is Mahara's **Find Groups** option.

Back to Janet to find out how she would like to use the **Find Groups** feature:

----- **Janet Norman form PI-Inc thinks** -----

I've heard that my colleague Fernando has created an interest group about allergy research. I'm really interested to see what's going on in this area because I hear there have been some recent breakthroughs. But, I don't know how to join the group to have a look at their forums. I need to know how to find and join the group I'm looking for.

Time for action – finding and joining a group

Let see how we can find the group for Janet and explore the ways in which we can search for a group we want to join:

1.   Under the **Groups** tab, click on the **Find Groups** option.

2.   The drop-down options display all the groups available under different categories. The default category is **Groups I'm not in** which is self-explanatory. To change categories, you can use the drop-down selector then click on the search icon (in this case a magnifying glass):

3.   Have a go at changing the search category and see what effect it has on the groups that are displayed below. If there aren't many groups in your site at this point then it is likely that some of the categories won't contain any groups. The other categories to choose from are **Groups I'm In** and **All groups**. When you have chosen your filter, click on the search button. For Janet, the **Groups I'm not in** drop-down reveals the group she is looking for:

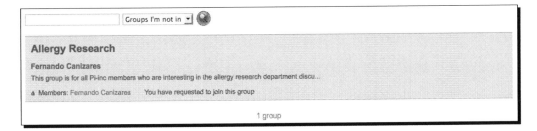

4. When your site starts getting really crowded with groups, it won't be enough to simply choose one of the categories and be able to find a specific group. You can improve your search by typing the group name in the search box provided before you click the magnifying glass, or equivalent, depending upon your Mahara site theme. Nevertheless, just for the experience of it, try searching now for one of the groups you have already created, or a group you are a member of, to see how the Mahara search functionality narrows it down to the one you actually want to see.

5. And that's it! That's all you need to know about searching through your groups.

What just happened?

We have just seen how easy it is to find groups in Mahara that we want to join.

As you are searching for a group, it will probably come to your attention just how important it is for people to set up a clearly named group title with a clear and useful description. For example, compare:

Group 1

Problems at work: Let's talk.

with

Group 2

Drilling, Milling, and Turning: In this group, we discuss practical techniques for working metal, sharing views, celebrating our work, and collecting and evaluating our best practice tips and ideas.

Hopefully you can see that the purpose of Group 2 is much more clear than Group 1.

Earlier we saw how to join an open membership group. Now let's look at how we can join *request membership* and *invite-only* groups. The process for joining these two group types requires a few extra steps but is no more difficult. Let's look at the request membership process.

Joining a request membership group

As you know, some groups require you to request membership. You will need to give a reason why you want to join the group and wait for the group administrator to accept you, if they think you are a suitable group member. The process for joining a group is:

1. You find a group you would like to request membership to.
2. You then request to join the group, indicating why you would like to join.
3. The group admin decides whether or not they would like you to join.

Time for action – requesting to join a group

Now let's have a look at the process in more detail:

1. Start by finding the group you would like to join. For this example, we will be using the **Allergy Research** group.

2. You will see that instead of a **Join this group** button, you have the **Request to join this group** option; click on it:

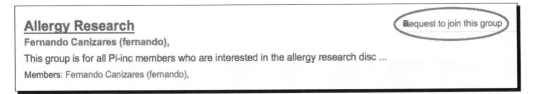

3. Next, you have a page that invites you to enter a description of why you want to join the group. Think carefully about what you will write in here. It is usually a good idea to give well-thought-out reasons for why you want to join as well as expressing enthusiasm for wanting to get involved. When you have given your reason, click **Request**:

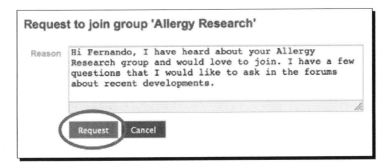

4. That's all there is to it! You have requested to join the group. You will see when you return to the group listing, that it now says **You have requested to join this group**.

What just happened?

You have just requested to join a group. Now, you must wait for the group administrator to decide whether or not you should be accepted.

Accepting/Denying requests to join a group

When someone has requested to join your group, you will see a message appear in the
Group | About page:

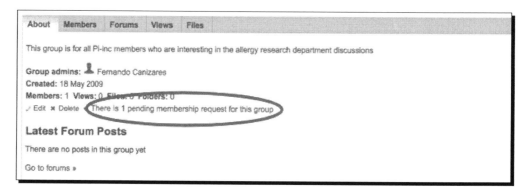

Click on that link. You will then see a page showing you who wants to join your group and the
reason why. If you are happy to add this new user, click the button to add the user.

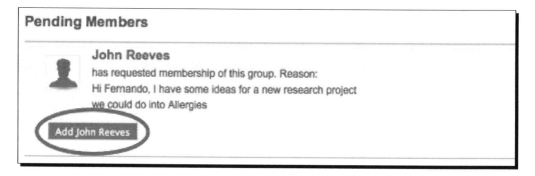

To finish this chapter we will have a look at how we can make friends in Mahara.

Making friends!

At the moment you will be feeling quite lonely in your site because you don't have any
friends! The Mahara friends feature allows you to find other people in the site that you
would like to connect with. Being someone's friend allows you to do a couple of important
things. Firstly, all your friends show up in your profile. This is a great way of being able to
quickly and easily find all the people in the Mahara site that you regularly contact. Secondly,
you can assign view access to your friends only. This is useful if you only want people you
know to be able to see one of the views you have created (as an alternative to making it
publicly available or available to all logged-in users.

Time for action – finding friends and adding them to your list

So, how do you find friends and add them to your network?

1. Return to the **Groups** section of your site and click on the **Find Friends** tab.

2. You will now see a page that lists all the people that are in your Mahara site. Notice in the top left you have the standard search box. Use this to search for the friend you are looking for if you can't see them in the list. When you have found the friend you would like to add, simply click **Send Friend Request** to the right of their name:

3. You have now requested to be someone's friend. You have to wait for their response before you are accepted as their friend.

What just happened?

You have just requested to be someone's friend.

Sometimes you may find that the person you want to add doesn't have the **Send Friend Request** option; instead it might say **Add to friends**. This is because that person is very sociable and has decided that they are happy for anyone to be their friend! When you click on one of those buttons, you automatically become that person's friend.

Similarly, you might find that there is no button there at all. That is because the person has decided that they don't want any friends. Instead, it will say **This user doesn't want any new friends**.

You can find out how to control who becomes your friend more closely in the next chapter.

Responding to a friend request

So how do you know when someone wants to be your friend? And what do you do if they do? Responding to a friend request is easy. You will spot that somebody has requested to be your friend from the main side block on your **Home** page:

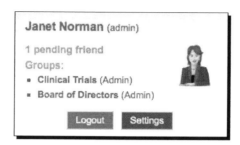

The message should read something like **1 pending friend** (or more). Click on that link to see who it is requesting to be your friend. If they sent you a message along with the request you will see that too. All you need to do now is to decide whether you want them to be your friend and, if so, to confirm them by clicking **Approve Request!**:

Managing your friends

When you start getting lots of friends, it will be useful for you to be able to filter through them and find someone you are looking for. To do this, you will be using the **My Friends** page. You may also want to remove a friend.

Time for action – filtering and removing friends

Let's find out how to do both:

1.   Return to the **Groups** section of your site and click on the **My Friends** tab.

2.   You will see a page that lists all your friends. Start by clicking on the drop-down box in the top-left corner shown below:

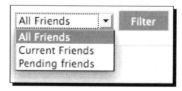

3. As you can see, there are three options for filtering your friends. You can choose to show all of your friends, both those who are confirmed and those who you have sent a request with the **All Friends** option. Alternatively, you might want to show just the friends that have definitely accepted your request and are now your friends with the **Current Friends** option. Finally, you can show all the friends who you are waiting to confirm your request by clicking **Pending Friends**. When you have decided which group you would like to see, click the **Filter** button.

4. You will now see all the friends that belong to that group. You will also see that for each friend there are two options. Click **Send message** to get in contact with your friend. If you no longer want to be someone's friend, click on the **Remove from friends** button.

5. When you choose to remove a friend, you get an option for explaining the reason for removing them; type in a reason and click **Remove friend.**

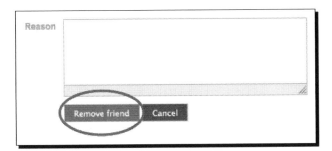

What just happened?

You have just learned how to view and filter through your friends, as well as how to remove friends from your list.

Whenever you send a message to a friend in Mahara, that message is found in your notifications section. We will be showing you how to read your notifications in the next chapter.

Summary

We learned a lot in this chapter about how we can be more social in Mahara by using the groups and friends features. Specifically, we looked at: creating groups, group types, forums and discussions, group views and files, and making friends.

We also discussed how we might use Mahara to encourage social interaction in our organization through sharing and discussion represented by our three fictional case study characters. Hopefully, now you have a good idea of how you can use the social facilities of Mahara to get people connecting and sharing ideas.

In the next chapter, we will be looking at how we can tailor our Mahara Portfolio using site settings and how to move our Portfolio around using the Mahara import/export facility.

6
Site Settings and Exporting Your Portfolio

You've now learned how to do lots of really useful things as a user in Mahara. In the next few chapters you will be looking at some more advanced features as you learn how to tweak Mahara to make it work better for you. Sensible new Mahara users will ideally sort out their site settings as soon as they join the site, a bit like reading the new TV manual before switching it on, but we thought that the first thing you would want to do is have a play. This chapter covers two major topics—site settings and export. In the former, we will be looking at how you can refine your Mahara portfolio to be more specifically tailored to your own needs, while in the latter, we will show you how you can export your portfolio so that it can be viewed as an HTML website and can be moved between Mahara and other ePortfolio systems.

In this chapter we shall:

- ◆ Set up your preferences
- ◆ Access your notifications
- ◆ Set up your activity preferences
- ◆ Export your portfolio to two different formats

Preferences

The site preferences page is the place in your portfolio that you can visit to fine-tune and personalize your system settings. You can control things such as your password, username, and other options. So let's change our site preferences.

Time for action – changing your preferences

1. Click on the **Settings** tab on the main menu.

2. You will automatically be on the page called **Preferences**. You have a number of options available. The first is to change your password. You may feel that you can't remember your old password very well and want to switch to a more memorable one. Try entering a new password for yourself. Enter your **Current Password** along with the **New Password** and a confirmation of your new password.

3. Next, you have the option to change your username. Perhaps your current username is too long and you would like to shorten it. Type in a **New username** for yourself. Ensure that you remember your new username. The username you choose must be available and not already taken by another user. Janet decided to change her username from **janet** to **jan**.

4. You will then see a group of **General Account** options. The first is to allow you to control who is your friend in the site. One idea is to set this to **New friends require my authorization.**

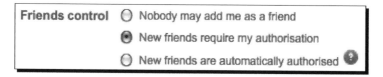

5. Leave the **HTML Editor** option set to **On** and **Messages from other users** set to **Allow anyone to send me messages**.

6. Switch the **Show controls to add and remove columns when editing a view** option to **On**. We will see what this does in the What just happened.

7. Make sure you click **Save** to make the changes.

What just happened?

You have just learned about the preferences that are available to you in your Mahara portfolio. You changed your username and password as well as a few of the more general options. Try logging in with your new username and password. Remember that if you want to change your username and password back to what they were originally, you can revisit your site settings.

Let's now look in more detail at each of the preferences we saw in the preceding section, thinking about why and when we would change our preferences.

Changing username and password

You should be sure about remembering new details before changing your username or password. You may need to change your password if you feel that you find it difficult to remember; perhaps you have a standard password for lots of online activities (for example, instant messaging/e-mail) and would like to use this for your Mahara too. Another good reason to change your password is because you have revealed it to someone else and now want to protect your own privacy.

Very rarely will you want to change your username. More often than not your username will have been set by your administrator and they are likely to have a naming system for all usernames in the site. It is best to check with your administrator before changing your username. One situation for changing a username may be that someone has left the institution who had a username that you wanted. For example, they may have had the username "sarah" and therefore you had to be "sarah1". Now that they have left, you can claim their username.

Friends control

We saw how to add friends in the last chapter, allowing you to gather all the people you know and recognize into a single group. The friends control here lets you choose how those people are able to become your friends. These are the available options:

- **Nobody may add me as a friend**: Select this option if you don't want anybody in the site to be able to add you as their friend. You may want to do this if you don't want to have to respond to friend requests all the time or don't want to use the friends feature in your portfolio. Perhaps you aren't interested in the social aspects of Mahara and simply want to build a portfolio.

- **New friends require my authorisation**: This is the option selected by default. By choosing this option you are allowing people to request to be your friend, but ultimately, it is up to you to decide whether they are accepted as one. This gives you some control over your friends in Mahara.

- **New friends are automatically authorised**: This means anyone in the Mahara can choose to become your friend without you having to allow them in. This option is for those of you who want elements of your portfolio to be more open and social. You have the option when you create a view, for example, to allow access to only friends. This would be useful for opening up elements of your portfolio to people who want to "follow" you, but not to all logged in users.

HTML editor

You can choose to use a **WYSIWYG (What You See Is What You Get)** editor in Mahara that makes your experience of typing into Mahara similar to that of using a basic word processor. It also gives you the ability to edit HTML code if you know how to do this. This gives you more flexibility when creating content in your portfolio. Some people switch this option off because they prefer to enter plain text. It's your choice.

Messages from other users

This allows you to control who is able to send you messages in Mahara. Here are the options:

- **Do not allow anyone to send me messages**: This means nobody can send/receive messages from you within the Mahara site. This option is for those who don't want to use Mahara socially and would rather receive messages via e-mail or other communication methods. It isn't advised to switch off messaging.

- **Allow people on my Friends list to send me messages**: This restricts those who can send you messages to just those on your friends list. This can be very useful if the Mahara site you are using has a lot of members and you don't want to receive unwanted mail from users that you don't know.

◆ **Allow anyone to send me messages**: This is the default option and places no restriction on who can message you. Use this option if you want to be more open and don't mind receiving messages from anyone within Mahara.

Show controls to add and remove columns when editing a view

When you are editing a Mahara view page, you will be adding in and taking away columns on your page as best you see fit. Turning this option on adds extra controls buttons, allowing you to add and remove columns as you are in the process of editing your view. If you leave it turned off, you will still be able to change your columns layout by using a drop-down box as we saw in Chapter 4. Here is what the new controls look like on the **Life in Tudor Times** view:

Use the **Add** buttons to add more columns to the right and left of the the current columns and **Remove** buttons to remove the column(s) below.

Maximum tags in cloud

Remember the tags feature we explained earlier? Well, this option simply allows you to restrict the number of tags that are allowed in the cloud sideblock. By default, the value is 20, which is a reasonable number. But you may find that you have lots of tags and would like to have more than 20 displayed. Similarly, you might want to restrict the number of tags displayed to just show the 10 most popular. The following image shows the differentiation in a cloud's appearance when it contains 10 tags compared to when it contains 20 tags:

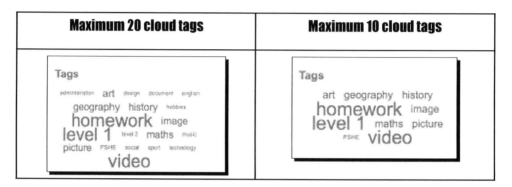

Maximum 20 cloud tags	Maximum 10 cloud tags

Preferences in the right sidebar

Another way to adjust your preferences without visiting this page it so use to **Preference** options that often appear in the right sidebar. For example, the **Friends control** options appear in the **My Friends** and **Find Friends** areas of the site. Here is the **Friends control** preference sidebar.

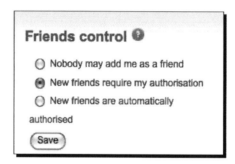

Notifications

In the last chapter we mentioned that you could receive messages telling you that posts have been added to a forum and you can receive messages from other users.

The notification section is the place in your portfolio where you can go to receive messages telling you that certain things have happened in the site. The notifications are a result of events that have happened and are relevant to you personally. Let's see how to view and filter our notifications:

Time for action – managing your notifications

1. Click **Notifications** on the **Settings** submenu.

2. You will now see a screen listing all your notifications, including their **Subject**, **Activity type**, and **Date** sent. If you are quite new to the site, it is likely that you don't have many (if any) notifications yet. Let's start by seeing what to do if you have a received a message from another user. Janet sees in her notification section that she has received a message from **Fernando Canizares**. Click on the message link to view it.

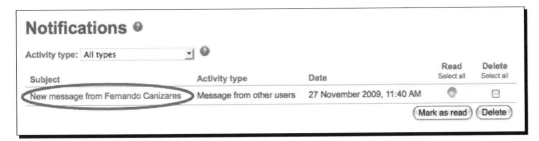

3. The message is then dropped down and displayed to you. Next, click the **More...** link.

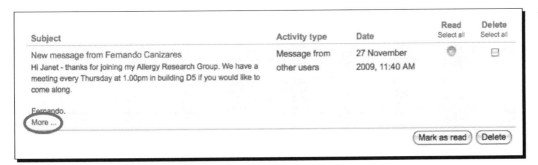

4. On this page, you will see that you have the option to reply to the message that you have been sent. Janet Norman replies to Fernando and clicks **Reply**.

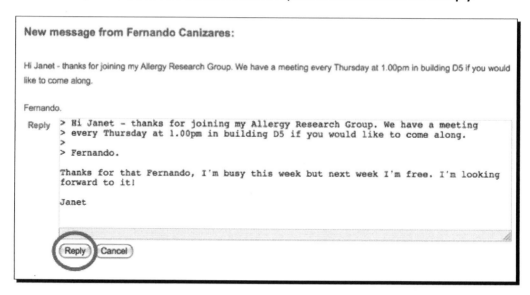

5. At this point you will find yourself in the **My Friends** area of the site, so navigate back to the **Notifications** area. Now that Janet has read the message from Fernando, she is going to delete it. To do that, check the box for the message in the **Delete** column. You can select more than one message to delete if you have lots of notifications that you want to remove. When you have selected the messages to delete, click the **Delete** button.

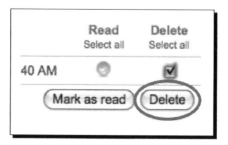

Note that you also have the **Mark as read** option for your notifications.

6. Finally, you also have the ability to filter your notifications by **Activity type**. Click on the drop-down box and try choosing one of the activity types to display all you notifications related to that **Activity type**.

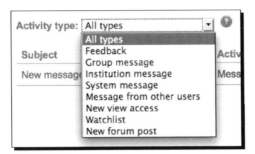

What just happened?

You just saw how to view, filter, and delete notifications. We saw that there are different activity types that cause notifications in Mahara. Let's have a look at each of these and understand what they mean:

- **Feedback**: These are the feedback comments that we saw in Chapter 4, and which you receive at the bottom of the views you have produced. Whenever you receive a feedback, it will appear in your notifications too.

- **Institution message**: In the next chapter we will be looking at what institutions are. These are messages sent to you by one of the administrators of an institution to which you belong.

- **System message**: Occasionally you may receive a system message. These are messages that are automatically generated by the Mahara system or are sent to you by one of the system administrators.

- **Message from other users**: This is the activity type we saw in the last example. These are messages sent to you by other users within the Mahara site. It is the main way apart from your profile wall of communicating with other users in Mahara.

- **New view access**: These are automated messages alerting you about the fact that you or your group have been given access to a new view that somebody has set up. They may also mean that you have now been awarded access to an existing non-public view.

- ◆ **Watchlist**: These are automated messages that tell you when a view you have added to a watchlist has been updated.

- ◆ **New forum post**: These are message postings that have been added to a forum set up in one of the groups you belong to.

It is a good idea to regularly visit your notifications page to see if you have any new messages.

Watchlist

You can use this feature to build up a list of views you like to "follow". You will then receive notifications when these views are updated with new and interesting information by the views' owners.

We saw in Chapter 4 how to add views to our watchlist in the footer of a view using the **Add View to watchlist** option.

Activity preferences

We have learned about all the different activity types. Now we are going to look at refining the settings for how we receive information about each of these.

There are 3 different ways of receiving notifications and we call them notification types. Here are the different ways you can receive notifications:

- ◆ **Activity log:** This means you will have to log in to view your news under the **Notifications** tab that you saw earlier in this chapter (no e-mail notifications).

- ◆ **E-mail digest:** This means you will get one message a day to your primary e-mail account telling you what has happened over the last 24 hours .

- ◆ **E-mail:** This means all messages related to this activity come thorough to your primary e-mail account.

Let's see how you would change the Notification type in Mahara:

Time for action – choosing your activity preferences

1. Access your activity preferences by clicking **Activity preferences** on the **Settings** submenu.

2. On this page, you will see all the activity types we looked at earlier. Currently, you will see that each one has the notification type set to **Email**.

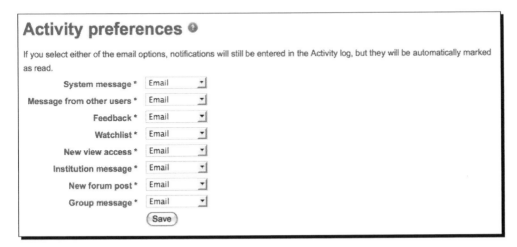

3. Change your **System message** setting from **Email** to **Activity log** using the drop-down box:

4. Click **Save** at the bottom of the page to make the change.

What just happened?

You have just personalized your activity preferences. Now let's think a bit more about those preference settings.

Let's have a look at a few different situations to help you understand these settings more clearly.

Punam from Pennytown Primary wants a fair bit of "hands-on" control over what her students are doing and wants a strong interface between her Mahara site and her e-mail account. Using the three notification types, she sets up her activity preferences like this:

Activity preferences ❷

If you select either of the email options, notifications will still be entered in the Activity log, but they will be automatically marked as read.

System message *	Activity log ▾
Message from other users *	Email ▾
Feedback *	Email digest ▾
Watchlist *	Email ▾
New view access *	Email ▾
Institution message *	Activity log ▾
New forum post *	Email digest ▾

Punam is not particularly interested in messages coming through either from her system administrators (the schools online people) or from her institution administrators (the Pennytown Primary administration office). She looks at the notifications area every now and then to check out activity logs from them. She isn't expecting her young learners to use the forums that often or to add much feedback to the views that she creates. A daily e-mail digest will be useful; however, just in case anything does crop up, she sets her **Feedback** and **New Forum** posts to **Email digest**.

However, Punam is going to insist that her learners have their own settings for new forum posts set up for them to receive individual e-mails. This is because Punam will use the forum to send them group messages and progress reports.

Punam will also give feedbacks individually on the views that the children create related to their project on the Tudors, so she will set the **Feedback** setting with her learners to individual e-mails.

Punam wants, together with her learners, to receive e-mail notifications when messages are sent from other users and also when changes are made to views that they have added to their watchlist. She is really pleased that Mahara offers the watchlist facility because it means she can closely monitor the work the learners are doing. She will be able to know when they make changes to their views.

Don't know what settings you want yet?

Don't worry, the decisions you make now are not going to be carved in stone and you can, indeed you regularly should, revisit this page and change your personal settings according to whatever is happening in your Mahara experience at the time.

Janet Norman from PI Inc is pleased that her users can configure their own settings. She thinks it is important that individual users get to choose for themselves how they interact with other system users and processes. Janet also recognizes that people in her company will want to change their settings on the go—choosing to receive regular e-mail notifications when they are busily engaged in a particular project and then cutting out those e-mail messages when they are focused on offline or more local issues.

For her own part, Janet has decided that she would prefer not to receive any e-mails or e-mail digests. She has decided to log in every day and check her **Notifications** tab for any news and changes. Janet's **Activity preferences**, therefore, look as shown in the following screenshot:

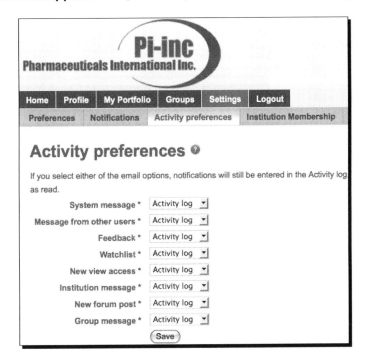

Before we move on, you may have noticed that there is also an **Institution Membership** tab in the settings area. Don't worry too much about this for now, we will be seeing what institutions are in the next chapter.

Pop quiz - activity types

Match the Activity type with its corresponding description:

System message	These are messages that are automatically generated by the Mahara System or are sent to you by one of the system administrators.
Messages from other users	These are automated messages that alert you or your group that access has been given to a new view that somebody has set up. They may also mean that you have now been awarded access to an existing non-public view.
Feedback	These are messages sent to you by one of the administrators of an institution you belong to.
Watchlist	These are messages sent to you by other users within the Mahara site.
New view access	These are automated messages that tell you when a view you have added to a watchlist has been updated.
Institution message	These are message postings that have been added to a forum set up in one of the groups you belong to.
New forum post	These are feedback comments that are posted at the bottom of Mahara views (or blogs/files) you have produced. (Not all views have to allow feedback.)

Have a go hero – play with different preference and settings

The more you get into using Mahara, the more you will understand how to set up the different preference settings and notification settings. For the first few weeks that you use Mahara, we advise you to experiment with different settings—for example, try turning on the view column controls and see if you like them. Experiment with the different ways the settings can be made to work for you.

Exporting your portfolio

A new feature introduced in Mahara 1.2 is the ability to export your Portfolio. This is a great feature because it means that your portfolio isn't trapped inside the Mahara website in which it resides; you can set it free whenever you want to! This is great news for your life-long learning. Work that you have done in one school, college, university, company, or other training provider can be transferred and developed upon as you move from institution to institution.

In Mahara, you currently have the ability to export your portfolio into the following two formats:

◆ **Standalone HTML website**: This option creates a self-contained website with your portfolio data. This means you can view your portfolio in a standard web browser such as Firefox, Safari, or Internet Explorer. This is great because it also means that you can easily show off your portfolio to others via your own website on the Internet rather than the Mahara owned by your educational institution.

◆ **LEAP2A**: This is a format that allows editable portfolios to be transferred from one portfolio system to another. This means you can not only move your portfolio between different Mahara sites, but also to and from any other ePortfolio system that supports this open format (for example, PebblePad `http://www.pebblepad.co.uk/`). Unlike the HTML format, LEAP2A is difficult to read for humans and should only be used for moving your portfolio around.

In the future, there may be more ways to export your portfolio. Let's see how you export your portfolio into the two formats using an example from Derrin Kent's portfolio.

Time for action – exporting your portfolio

1. Under the **My Portfolio** tab on the main menu, click on **Export**.

2. On this page, you will see the two options for exporting your portfolio. Let's start by making a standalone HTML website. Make sure the **Standalone HTML Website** option is selected (it should be by default).

3. Next, you have the choice of exporting your entire portfolio, or just one or more views. Let's export just one of Derrin's views to be displayed as an HTML web page. To do this, first click on the **Just some of my Views** link under **What do you want to export?**

4. You will see a section drop down that invites you to choose which views you would like to export. Derrin chooses his **Free Software for Education** view and checks the box next to it in order to select it.

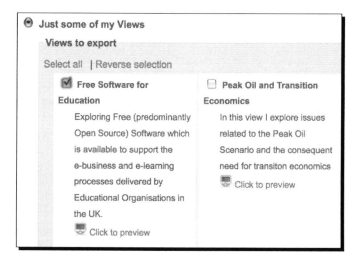

Remember, you can choose as many views as you would like to export.

5. To do the export, click on the **Generate Export** link at the bottom of the page. You will see a progress bar telling you the details of the export as it is in progress. When finished, you will see a dialogue box inviting you to save or unzip the file that was created.

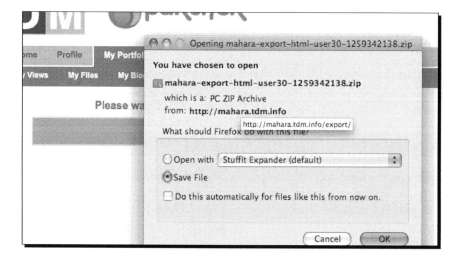

6. Now, let's have a look at the file we just created. It will be a ZIP file, so before you do anything else, you will need to decompress it. When you have done that you should see a folder named something similar to `portfolio-for-Derrin` but with your username on the end. Open the folder and you will see all the contents of your export. To view your new website, click on the `index.html` file in the folder. Here is what Derrin's view looks like as a web page:

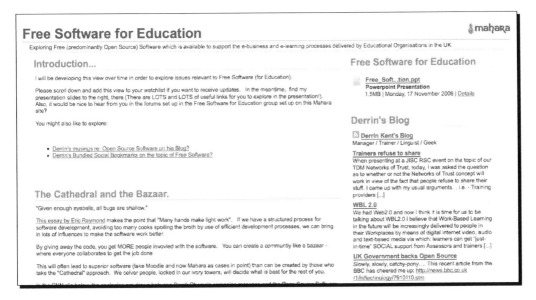

7. We've exported and viewed our portfolio as a web page, now let's export our portfolio to LEAP2A format. Return to the **Export** page in your portfolio. This time, select the **LEAP2A** option and generate the export. You will be asked to save the result in the same way that you did with the HTML website export.

8. This time, once unzipped, your export will be named something similar to `mahara-export-leap-user1-1259342849 Folder`.

9. That's it! You've just exported your portfolio to two different formats using Mahara's export facility.

What just happened?

We just exported our portfolio to both a standalone HTML website and LEAP2A format.

HTML website export

The HyperText Markup Language is the most common language used on the Internet. The option to download to this format allows you to keep a copy of your own work on your own computer and view it whenever you want to with your favorite internet browser. You could even have your own webpage, nowadays it has become incredibly cheap to rent some web space on a web server—just Google "cheap web hosting".

LEAP2A export

LEAP2A is an open format that doesn't belong to any company or individual. In an age where data is commonly and perhaps sometimes inappropriately being used by large organizations and governments, it is good to think that we can maintain control over our own learning data. With the LEAP2A format it will always be available for us to use.

Another good thing about this format is that many ePortfolio systems are adopting it. Not only can you move your own stuff from one Mahara site to another, but also between different ePortfolio products.

You are probably wondering how you can import your LEAP2A data from another Mahara system into this one. You can't do this by yourself—the system administrator has to do this for you.

Pop quiz – Export

A student is moving from one school to another, both schools have a Mahara ePortfolio system. The student would like to take their portfolio with them when they move; which format should they export their Portfolio to?

Have a go hero – Show off your portfolio by exporting to HTML website

Try using the HTML export function to create yourself a standalone version of your portfolio. You now have a simple but effective way of creating your own website and showing it off to others. If you're feeling adventurous, you could learn some basic HTML and CSS to tweak the resultant website to be more presentable. The best place to start learning HTML and CSS is http://www.w3schools.com/.

Summary

In this chapter, you learned about some of the more advanced things you can do with your portfolio. Specifically, you saw how to set up your Site Preferences, which allows you to edit parts of your portfolio such as your own username and password. You also started managing your notifications, learning how to edit where you want your notifications to go to and what you want to receive notifications for. You learned about the watchlist, what it is and why you would use it as well as adjusting you own activity preferences. Finally you exported your portfolio into a couple of different formats to allow you to both display it in a web browser or to upload it to a different Mahara system.

In the next chapter, we will be looking at some advanced roles in Mahara, including institutional administrators, staff members, and group tutors.

7
Institution Administrators, Staff Members, and Group Tutors

So far, we've looked at how we can use all the standard features of Mahara to put together our own eye-catching portfolio, socialize with other Mahara users, and control our settings. In this chapter we are going to look at roles beyond that of a standard user.

In the first part of the chapter, we will look at institutions using Mahara and some of the things that an Institutional Administrator can do.

The second part will focus on using Mahara specifically within a learning context, where there is more of a need for teachers/tutors to manage students/ learners. We will be exploring a special type of Group called a Course Group. We will also be looking at two types of roles associated with these groups called "staff members" and "group tutors".

In this chapter we shall:

◆ Explore the options available to an Institutional Administrator for managing members, including how to set up staff members in your Institution

◆ As a staff member, find out how to set up a special controlled group, to which members can submit work as assignments

◆ Discover what a group tutor can do and how to create one

◆ Learn how to submit work to and release work from a controlled group

◆ See a practical example of using controlled groups for assessment of learners' work

What is an institution?

An Institution is a sub-division of a Mahara site, which can have its own administrators. The three main advantages of using Institutions are:

◆ Rather than having a number of separate Mahara installations, a consortium of different institutions can share a common user base on a single Mahara site. This allows users to network with others across institutional boundaries.

◆ A Mahara Site Administrator can devolve much of the responsibility for user management to Institutional Administrators.

◆ Each institution can be given its own theme.

For example, a group of schools working together in a local area may wish to share a single Mahara installation. This may be because students naturally migrate from one school to another but want to retain continuity in their lifelong learning. It may be because a teacher of a particular subject teaches learners from a variety of schools. Finally, it could be that the schools have seen the advantage of encouraging common interest groups across the region (for example, chess/sports/music groups).

While the local area wants to promote collaboration between the schools, each school will want to retain control over its users. They will also want the users from their own school to be clearly identified as they operate within the Mahara site. Even on a shared Mahara platform, each institution can achieve this "localization" by having its own look-and-feel with its own institutional theme.

----- **Punam from Pennytown Primary thinks** -----

Pennytown Primary has been set up as one of the many institutions within the Schools Online Mahara Site. We have our own school theme, which the site administrators have created for us. Other schools in our local area also have their own themes. I, personally, have not been set up as the Institutional Administrator for Pennytown Primary. These permissions have been set up for one of the school administrators called Susan. I have to advise Susan when I want a new institutional member to be added.

Institutional theming, though, is an option, not a necessity. Many organizations prefer to keep a common theme across the whole site but still subdivide into Institutions simply because they wish to defer user management responsibilities to those people who have more everyday contact with the local Mahara users.

----- **Janet Norman form PI-Inc thinks** -----

At PI Inc, it makes sense for us to have an Institutional Administrator for each and every branch. This way somebody with their fingers on the local pulse can maintain the institutional user membership and keep it live and current. I thought about giving each branch its own theme, but I decided against it. This is because, at the end of the day, PI Inc is an international brand and it is unnecessary to distinguish between the different branches in different cities around the world.

Administering an institution

An Institutional Administrator only needs to deal with members in their own institution. An Institutional Administrator may be responsible for the following:

- Configuring institutional settings
- Managing new user subscriptions and dealing with requests to join the institution
- Removing, suspending, and reactivating users
- Monitoring abusive behavior in the institution
- Allocating institutional themes
- Deciding what information users of their institution will provide as a minimum when joining up
- Allocating roles to staff members and to other Administrators of the institution

Let's find out how you can manage your institution. To follow the tasks in this section, your Mahara Site Administrator has to have set you up as an Institutional Administrator. Once he/she has done this, then you will be able to control the membership of your institution and your institutional settings by yourself. Let's start by seeing how we can add new users to your institution.

Time for action – adding users to your institution

1. Log into your Mahara as an Institutional Administrator. (If you do not have these permissions, ask your Site Administrator to give them to you. They may need to set up a new site institution for you to work with.) Once you have these permissions, you will see that you have a new tab called **User Administration**.

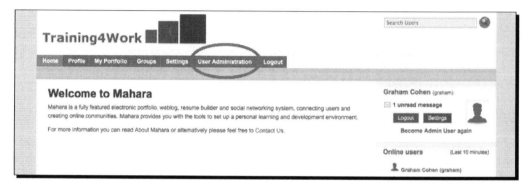

2. Click the **User Administration** tab. You have now entered the User Administration area of your Mahara site:

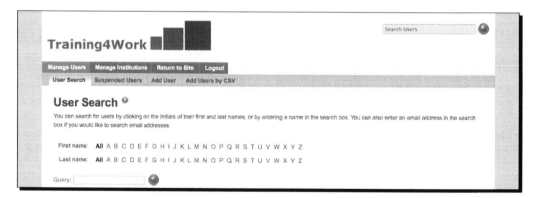

3. Here, you are able to control the users and settings for your own institution. You can return to the main Mahara site whenever you want to by clicking the tab **Return to Site**. Though don't do that right now, we have work to do in here, first.

        ❑   You will see that the **Manage Users** tab is selected. Let's explore the sub-menu options that you can see on this page. By default you will be on the **User Search** page. This is page will be extremely useful for us later. But, before we do anything else, we are going to start by adding some users to our new institution. Click on the **Add User** sub-menu item. You will see a screen that looks as follows:

❑ You will see that the **Add User** page has three sections. Start by looking at section **User Creation Method**. In this section you can decide how your users are created. You can **Create a new user from scratch** or **Upload LEAP2A File**. Use the radio button to decide which option to use. We saw in Chapter 6 how the LEAP2A files can be used to import portfolio information. For now, you will probably want to create a brand new user. Enter their name and e-mail address. Graham has decided to add a new user called **Peter Tooley** to his institution:

      ❑   In **Basic Details,** add a **Username** and **Password** for your user. The user will be invited to change the password when they log in for the first time, so make sure you remember the password you gave them. You are also allowed to change the **File quota** for their use. This setting controls how much space they have to upload files in their Mahara area. It is probably best to talk to the Site Administrator before changing this. You also have the option to make the user an Institutional Administrator like yourself. Graham has made Peter Tooley into a standard user and given him a username and password:

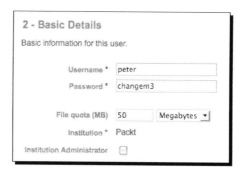

      ❑   Finally, in **Create**, simply click the **Create User** button.

And that's how easy it is. You will now see a page displaying the site settings for your new user. We will see what each of these options means later in the chapter.

What just happened?

We have just learned how to add users to our institution. Hopefully, you will now have some users in your institution.

When you made your user, you had to allocate them a username and password. It is a good idea to keep the naming scheme for your users consistent across the whole institution. One simple scheme would be to use the first name of your users as the username. For example, Peter Tooley would have the username **peter**. When you want to add another user with the same first name you could just append a number to the end, like **peter2**. Another method would be to use both first name and surname in the username, so Peter Tooley's username would now be **peter.tooley**. This method would reduce the likelihood of having to use many numbers because there would be less chance of duplication.

When you allocate your users a password you should be aware that they will be changing it when they first log in. It is a good idea to give all of your users the same password for them to log in the first time—this way you will remember it.

Bulk uploading users to your institution

When administering your institution, you also have the option to bulk upload users by CSV. **CSV** stand for **Comma-Separated Values**. This simply means that you can set up multiple users in one single action by uploading a simple text file that you have created. This text file will list many of your users and identify their particular attributes. This CSV file "trick" will save you time if you have multiple users to upload into your institution.

Time for action – adding institutional users by CSV

1. Click on the **Add Users by CSV** tab in the **Manage Users** sub-menu. On this page you will get to read some useful instructions explaining how you should set up your CSV file.

2. There will be at least five mandatory fields for a CSV file. As an Institutional Administrator you may have set up more mandatory fields for your institution (we will see how to do this in the *Configuring your institution's settings* section of this chapter) If so, your CSV file will also need to include a reference for these fields for each learner.

3. You are wisest to create your CSV files in a plain text-editing software application, such as "Notepad" on Windows, "TextEdit" on a Mac or "Gedit" for Linux. Imagining that you had locked the additional field for **city** in your institution, an example CSV file on a Mac might look as follows:

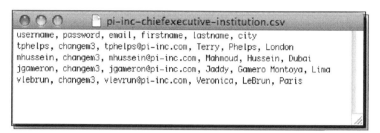

4. Now make a CSV file of your own for some users you would like to upload and save it to your computer.

5. Use the **Browse** button to the find the CSV file that you have created on your computer. (Many people save their CSV files somewhere on their web server. This is not a very secure thing to do and we strongly advise against it.)

6. Make the decision whether you wish to force a password change and whether you wish to send an e-mail alert to new users telling them they have been added to the system. When you are ready, click the button to **Add Users by CSV**:

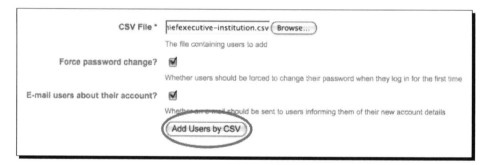

What just happened?

You have just used a CSV file to set up new users in bulk for your Mahara Institution.

Editing user account settings

By now you have begun to add some users to your institution, but you may want to go back and change some of the details that you entered when you first created them. You can do this using the **User Account Settings** section. Each user in your institution has their own Account Settings.

These Account Settings are subdivided into three sections—each with configurable options for your user:

◆ Site Account Settings

◆ Suspend/Delete User

◆ Institution Settings

The **Site Account Settings** allow you to create a new password for your user. This comes in handy later when your users forget their old one. It is also useful to notice that you can set an account expiry date and that you can reconfigure the user's **File quota** limit.

You can also suspend a user using the option to **Suspend/Delete User**. Suspending the user has the effect of stopping them from logging into and using the Mahara system. There are many reasons as to why you might do this, ranging from response to inappropriate behavior through non-payment of user fees (some organizations charge their clients to use Mahara) to termination of a paid course. Whatever your reason, it is a good idea to use the text entry box provided to explain to the user exactly why their access has been suspended the next time they try to log in. Once you have suspended a user, you can delete them completely by clicking the **Suspended Users** button. Select the checkboxes for all the users you wish to erase and then click the button to **Delete Users**. You will naturally receive a warning asking you if you are sure you want to take this (drastic and irreversible) action before you take it. If you are sure you are doing the right thing, go ahead and delete these users permanently.

----- Janet Norman form PI-Inc thinks -----

I like the Institutional Administrators to have the powers to delete a user if they choose to, but I actually encourage them to do no more than suspend these users from their institution. This is partly because when an employee leaves one PI Inc branch they might be moving to another one of our branches, or act as an external consultant, and it is much easier to unsuspend them than to create them and their portfolio from scratch all over again.

Finally, you can set **Institution Settings** for your user. You will notice here that you can choose to automatically expire a user's membership of your institution at a certain point in time. You may also choose to give the learner an ID number within your institution. The final thing to note is that you can use this page to turn a particular user into an Institutional Administrator (the same as you) or alternatively set them up as an Institutional Staff Member. We will look at the type of things a staff member can do later on in this chapter.

Let's look in more detail at how to suspend/delete users in our Institution:

Time for action – finding a user and suspending them

1. Start by searching for the user that you would like to suspend. Click on the **Manage Users** main menu tab, then on **User Search**.

2. On this page, you will see all the users in your institution listed. You can search alphabetically, or by typing a query in the search box. Find the user you are looking for and click on their name.

3. This will link you to their **Account Settings** page. As we discussed earlier, this page is split into three sections. To suspend a user, look in the middle section entitled **Suspend/Delete User**. To suspend your user, type a reason in the box and click **Suspend User**.

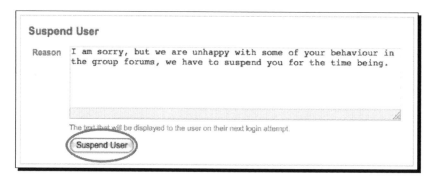

That's all there is to it. You have just suspended the user. Now, visit the **Suspended Users** page of the admin area by clicking on **Manage Users** on the main menu, then click on **Suspended Users**. This page displays all the users that have been suspended. You have the option on this page to **Unsuspend Users** or to go on to delete them from the Mahara system. To do this, just click in the select box to the right of the user's name and click **Unsuspend Users** or **Delete Users**. I am going to unsuspend the user in this example because they have now promised to improve their behavior in the forums.

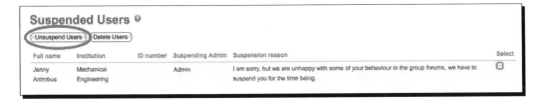

What just happened?

You have just learned how to find users in your institution and to suspend and delete or unsuspend them.

It is important to know when you should suspend a user. You should have a good reason before you suspend somebody because it could be potentially disturbing to their work and personal reflection. Not only that, but someone may feel offended if you suspend them without a good cause. Users are usually suspended if they are displaying poor behavior to other users throughout the system, through groups and forums. Other bad behavior of a user may be that they have allowed someone else log in as them and to unfairly alter their ePortfolio. Whatever the problem though, think carefully over whether you want to suspend or even delete a user from the system.

Masquerading as another user

It is worth drawing your attention to the fact here that, as an Institutional Administrator, you can also choose to "Masquerade" as one of the Mahara users in your institution. As we have just pointed out it feels, in principle, wrong and unfair to use such a privilege to edit another person's ePortfolio work. However, there can sometimes be good reasons for us to choose to masquerade.

Perhaps we would want to set new learners up with the skeleton file structure and copy views they would need. You could masquerade in order to set learners up in this way during a formalized stage within an organization's user setup process. Alternatively, maybe you have had a complaint about a user and need to investigate what is happening in their learning space?

Whatever your ethical and decent reason for doing so may be, if you want to masquerade as another Mahara user, you should go first to the users' **Site Account Settings** page. Next, look under the user's avatar located to the top-left of your screen. You will see the clickable option to **Login as <Username>**.

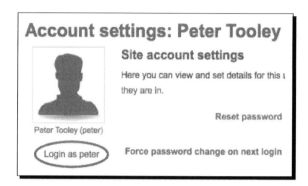

No need to change the user's password at this point (although do notice that you could if you chose to). Instead, for now, just click the link to **log in anyway**.

You will now find yourself masquerading as that particular user.

Whenever you are ready to finish your masquerade, click the banner at the top of the screen, which gives you the option to become the Institutional Administrator again:

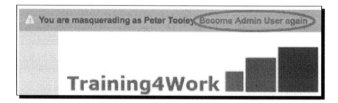

Managing member roles in your institution

Moving people in and out of the Member, Institution Staff, and Institution Administrator statuses of your Institution couldn't be easier. Let's look at:

- ◆ How we can manage our Institution Members, including how to delete users and respond to requests to join your institution
- ◆ How we can make Members into Institutional Staff
- ◆ How we can make Members into Institutional Administrators

Time for action – managing your institution's members, staff and admins

1. We saw in Chapter 6 that site members are able to request to join an institution using their Site Settings (provided that the institution allows users to register themselves in this way). As an Institutional Administrator, you can respond to these requests deciding whether or not you would like that user to join you. Start by clicking on **Manage Institutions | Members**. You will see a page similar to the following screenshot:

2. On this page, you can do three things with your members; respond to requests to join your institution, invite people to join your institution, or delete members. This is controlled by the drop-down box called **Users to display**.

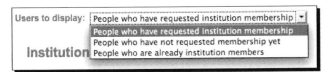

3. As you can see, the current selection is **People who have requested institution membership**. You will see members displayed who have requested to join. To accept the new member, first click on their name, then click on the right-hand arrow to move them across to the **Users to be added/rejected** area.

 Moving more than one user at a time

Shift + click to select a large block of users for moving across in one go and *Ctrl* + click to select multiple users in various positions on your list in order to move them with one single click of the arrows.

4. You will now see that the user has moved to the right-hand side section called **Users to be added/rejected**. To finish, click **Add members**. Alternatively you may have wanted to decline the person, in which case you would click **Decline requests**.

5. This format for managing your users is the same for the other two options in the drop-down box we saw in step 2. Try inviting some users to join your institution using the **People who have not requested membership yet** drop-down option.

6. To manager who is set to be a Staff Member in your institution, click on the **Institution Staff** sub-menu option of the **Manage Institutions** section.

7. You will see a page very similar to the one you used to manage your members. Following the same procedure of using the arrows to move your members to the staff section, you can then submit these members to be staff in the institution.

8. Finally, you can manage your Administrators in the same way using the **Institution Administrators** sub-menu tab. On this page, you can decide who should or shouldn't be an Administrator for your institution.

What just happened?

We have just seen how we can manage the roles for people in our institution.

One thing we looked at was how to turn a user into a Staff Member in the institution. An Institutional Staff Member is simply a person in your institution who has the ability to create and administer Course Groups. (We will find out more about these later in the chapter.)

Configuring your institution's settings

Now that we've looked at our Institution's Members and their settings let's move on to configuring the settings for the institution. To find your Institutional Settings, click **Manage Institutions** on the main menu. You will find yourself, by default, on the Settings page, which looks something as follows:

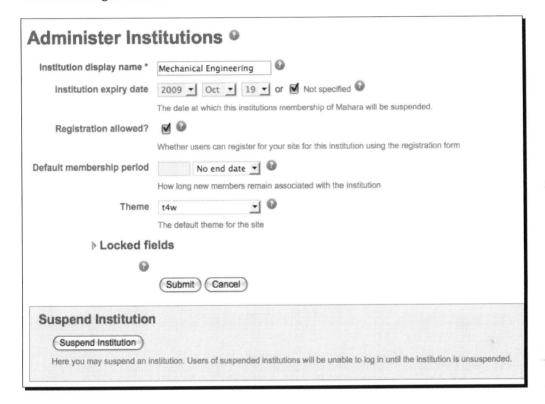

Firstly, you can edit your Institution's display name here to another name if you prefer to.

You can set an **Institution expiry date** here if you wish to. You might do this if, for example, you have set up a short-term institution for a particular conference event or for an event on your social calendar.

You may be interested to see the checkbox option asking if you wish to set **Registration allowed?** If you set this, you are allowing users to register themselves as a member of your institution using a registration form. This option is wisely left unchecked by default. Most people will prefer to decide for themselves who becomes a member of their institution rather than letting people to register for themselves.

You can set the number of days, weeks, months, or even years you might wish to allow members to access your site for. For example, a university offering a three year undergraduate degree program might set a membership of a Mahara degree course institution to four years. They would then explicitly advise their new cohort of students that they will be able to access the content of their Mahara ePortfolios for one year (only) beyond the termination of their degree program.

This is also the page where you can determine the **Theme** your Institutional Users view when accessing the Mahara site. Use the drop-down box here to choose your favored theme. By default, Mahara provides a range of themes to choose from including Default, Aqua, Fresh, Raw, Sunset, and Ultima. It is highly likely, though, that your Mahara Site Administrator will have created some site-specific themes, from which you will be able to select.

You may wish to lock some user data fields for your institution by using the arrow icon to the left of the words **Locked Fields**. This means, for example, that you can force your institutional members to supply you with their home phone number or the city/region where they are based. By default, the mandatory fields a Mahara user has to supply are only their username, password, e-mail, First Name, and Last Name fields. If you want to insist you get more than this when users register for your institution, this is your opportunity. Go ahead and check some of those checkboxes.

The final (very prominent) option for you to notice on this page is the option to **Suspend Institution**. If you choose to do this, you will be disallowing your institution members from logging into your Mahara site. This is, hopefully, not something you will be likely to do very often! You may choose to do this while you are setting up the initial infrastructure of groups, views, and files you will be using in a new institution that you are establishing.

Dealing with admin notifications

As an Institution Administrator you will have the responsibility to respond to user activities within the site. Under the **Admin Notifications** tab, you will see that you will be advised about, and have the chance to respond to, the following circumstances:

- ◆ **Contact Us**: A user has made contact with you via the Contact Us facility. (This facility is always easily accessed by looking at the footer of your Mahara page—even when logged out.)

◆ **Objectionable Content**: At the bottom of user submitted views, reading users will find the option to **Report Objectionable Content to the Mahara Administrators**. You will receive notifications on this page when this happens. You will then need to go ahead and investigate the incident reported. While inappropriate behavior can't be completely thwarted on a Mahara site, in just the same way as you cannot stop this sort of thing from happening in a real-world environment, you can at least use this facility to responsively investigate any reported incidents. Furthermore, you almost certainly wouldn't be able to get as clear an understanding of what was actually said in a real-life incident as you might be able to see when investigating an incident that has occurred in Mahara.

◆ **Repeat virus upload and Virus flag release**: Unfortunately, some users are not as careful with protecting their computers from viruses as they should be. Mahara has a facility that can spot files which have been affected by any viruses. If an infected file is identified, Mahara will disallow the user from submitting the file, requesting that they run the file through an anti-virus application before resubmitting. Repeat attempts to upload files containing viruses will be brought to your attention as an Institution Administrator on this page. It is up to you to release files that have been flagged with a virus or to suspend user accounts in cases of regularly repeated virus issues as best you see fit.

Institution views and files

You can set up Mahara Views and Files that pertain to your particular institution.

Views

Click on the **Views** tab and then click the **Create View** button. You will notice that you have the tabs to drag and add blocks for **External Feeds**, **Files, images and video,** and the **General** options. But you do not see the options to add blocks from your Profile, your Resume, nor for your Blogs.

This is simply because these latter tabs represent more personalized content. The institution views are intended to carry person-neutral content, representing more generic content that can be made available to institution members. Should one of these views be made copyable, of course, any user can then go on to add more personalized views to the view they create from this institutional view, which has been provided as a starting point, should they wish to.

Otherwise, the setting up of an Institutional View follows much the same process as that of setting up a view for yourself as a user. One useful additional functionality you might appreciate is the option to **Copy for new institution members**—an option that only becomes available after the **Allow copying** box has been checked.

> Allow copying ☑
>
> Check this box if you would like the people who can see your view to be able to make their own copies of it.
>
> Copy for new Institution members ☐
>
> Automatically make a personal copy of this View for all new members of Mechanical Engineering.

The important point to note here is that only new and not existing members of your institution will receive this editable view automatically. You will have to get existing users to copy it for themselves if you want them to have it (unless you are willing to start masquerading as the users in order to do the copying work for them yourself).

With a bit of sensible and strategic forward planning, when you set up your new institution, you can use this **Copy for new institution members** facility to set up some templates. For example, a learner could then bounce off these templates when they are submitting work to be assessed for an evidence-based or project-based qualification.

You could also use this facility to create non-assessed generic content, which all new members of your institution may find useful. An institution for gardeners, for example, might have added a "task-list" textbox into a view that illustrates annual gardening tasks. The individual users could then select and reject from this textbox provided in order to create their own, personalized annual timetable of gardening tasks.

Files

The files you upload into your institution will be available for use by all of your institution members. Files uploaded here could be general information documents that you would like the whole Institution to read, such as the site code for practice or a simple user guide.

Let's move on, now, to consider why we would use Course Groups, Staff Members, and Course Tutors in Mahara.

Pop quiz – managing an institution

- Sometimes uploading one user at a time can take too long, especially when you have a list of over a hundred. If I were an Institutional Administrator, what type of file could I use to make life easier for myself?

- Name three things that an Institutional Administrator can do to manage their users.

- What does **Suspending your Institution** do?

Less learner-driven aspects of Mahara

For the rest of this chapter, we will look at Mahara from a learning context. In this context, it is important for all of us to see a Mahara site as a space where learners who own their own personalized learning materials can choose whether or not to allow others to access them. The individual learner can also choose whether or not to interact with other site users in reference to the materials they create. Mahara is very much to be perceived as a learner-driven environment.

However, this does not mean that there is no useful role for an administrator or tutor in such an environment. Here are some of the things that a tutor might want to do in an ePortfolio system:

- Monitor their learners work, ready to give feedback on it

- Decide who's in and who's out of particular areas of the site

- Scaffold learners' work by creating templates, which they can work from and go on to extend creatively

- Get work submitted to them for formal assessment

- Allow other to access assessable work, such as teaching assistants, inspectors, or other types of verifiers

Mahara has provided the features needed to achieve all of the above.

In Neil's case, there are clear reasons for him to want to exert some control over the learning process. He wants to give some of his colleagues a way to supervise and structure the work their learners are doing. In this chapter, we will look at how Neil can use Mahara to meet his particular needs. We hope to get you thinking about how you might want to use Mahara in different institutions, for the delivery of formally assessed programs, and for monitoring project-based or evidence-based learning.

----- **Neil from Training 4 Work thinks** -----

I have a colleague called Graham, also an engineer, who has now become interested in using Mahara for his own cohort of mechanical engineering students. My own students are studying electrical engineering courses. I would like to be able to allow Graham to manage his own users in his own section of Mahara.

Neither Graham nor I would ever want to inhibit our learners' creative and personalized learning process. However, we do feel a need to manage some aspects of our users' work in a more formal and assessment-driven way. We would like our learners to submit some of their work to us "For Assessment". We will need to give feedback on this work and direct them further until it meets the standards we need. Once it has reached the required standards we will need to give access to the learners' work to an external verifier from an accrediting body.

What is a course group?

We covered standard Mahara groups extensively in Chapter 5 of this book. There is, though, another type of group within Mahara, which can only be set up by Mahara Administrators (either Site Administrators or Institution Administrators) and/or by Mahara Staff Members. These groups allow for more formalized assessment processes and are known in Mahara as Course Groups.

There are two types of Staff Members within Mahara—Site Staff Members and Institutional Staff Members. We have seen so far in this chapter how we can set up an Institutional Staff Member, but there is absolutely no difference between the Institutional and Site Staff Member types.

The Mahara site itself (before any institutions are set up) is probably best thought of as an institution in its own right. In fact, the Mahara system refers to the Site Level institution as "No Institution". This "No Institution" is (counter-intuitively) a Mahara institution itself. No Institution is the name given to the top-level Institution of a Mahara site.

Anyhow, whether they are in the site-level institution (that is, No Institution) or in another institution, what is it that a Staff Member can do, which other site users/institution members can't? You may remember that in Chapter 5 when we were looking at group types we didn't go into detail about the course group type? Well, you've been waiting for it, here we go...

The main difference is that with course groups we can do the following:

♦ Group owners can create Tutors for these groups.

♦ Users can submit work for assessment by the tutors in this group. Tutors can then give feedback on any views submitted, adding files as part of their feedback if they need to. This tutor feedback can be restricted to the viewing of the view owner only.

But, there are three extra types of groups available to Administrators and Staff members, two Course Groups, and one additional Standard Group.

♦ **Course: Request membership groups** where users themselves have to request to join your group. Once you have accepted them into your course group, these users will be enabled to submit views for your assessment.

♦ **Course: Controlled membership groups** where you as the group owner can search for users and then go to their profile page in order to add them to your group yourself. The advantage of this type of group is that you can decide for yourself who gets added to your course group. The users themselves are left with no option but to be included.

♦ **Standard: Controlled membership groups** where, although the group owner still gets to choose who is in and who is out of their own group, the options to add group tutors and to have users submit their work for assessment are not made available.

The relationship between the different Mahara group types can be represented in a table:

		Standard Groups				Course Groups	
		Open Membership	Invite Only	Request Membership	Controlled Membership	Request Membership	Controlled Membership
Member Enrollment	Anyone can join up whenever they like	✓	✗	✗	✗	✗	✗
	Only invited people can join – IF they decide to accept your invitation	✗	✓	✗	✗	✗	✗
	People have to have their own decision to "Request Membership" approved by you before they can join	✗	✗	✓	✗	✓	✗

		Standard Groups				Course Groups	
		Open Membership	Invite Only	Request Membership	Controlled Membership	Request Membership	Controlled Membership
Moderation and Assessment	The group owner can "force" people to become members of this group	x	x	x	✓	x	✓
	The group owner can set up Forum Moderators for this group	✓	✓	✓	✓	✓	✓
	The group owner can set up Tutors for this Course Group	x	x	x	x	✓	✓
	Group members can submit their views "For Assessment" by the Course Tutors	x	x	x	x	✓	✓
	Course Tutors can give private feedback (including and attached file) to Views Submitted "For Assessment"	x	x	x	x	✓	✓

 The three gray columns indicate the group types that only Administrators and Staff Members have the privileges to set up.

----- **Punam from Pennytown Primary thinks** -----

Although Susan, the Pennytown Primary Institutional Administrator has had to set up the new learners for our school, I still get to maintain complete control over my own English Tudor Monarchy Group's membership and permissions. This is because I have been set up as a Staff Member in my school's institution (only) on our Mahara site. As I set up this particular Course: Controlled Membership group myself, I am in complete control of my class' English Tudor Monarchy Group. I am allowed to set up other Group Administrators, Group Tutors, or Forum Moderators for this group, should I wish to.

Case study

Returning to our example from Training 4 Work, Graham has now made the user he created earlier, Peter Tooley, into a Staff Member. Peter is the course leader for an evidence-based qualification (for example NVQ Level 2 in the UK) in Mechanical Engineering, which is why he belongs in this Institution. He and his tutors would like to be able to assess evidence submitted by the learners through Mahara. We will now learn how Peter can set this up in Mahara.

We'll start out by seeing how a Staff Member can set up a controlled membership group.

Time for action – setting up a Course: Controlled Membership group

You must be set up either as a Staff Member or as an Administrator in your Mahara site or a Mahara institution, in order to complete this *Time for action*. If you do not have these permissions, ask your Site Administrator, or your own Institution Administrator to set you up with the permissions you need. You are going to set up your first Course: Controlled Membership group.

1. Log in to your Mahara as either a general staff member or a staff member of an institution.

2. Click on the **Groups** tab in the main navigation bar.

3. On the **My Groups** page, click the **Create Group** button.

4. Create your group in exactly the same way that you did in Chapter 5, giving it a relevant name and description. This time, however, choose the **Course: Controlled Membership** group type. Here are the settings for the group created by Peter Tooley, the Staff Member that Graham added to his institution earlier in this chapter.

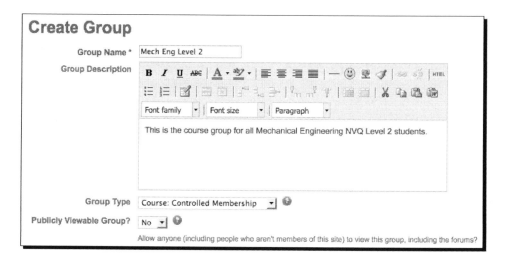

5. Click **Save Group** to finish!

And that's all there is to it. We now have a course group ready for learners to submit views to.

What just happened?

We just learned how to make our own course group as a Staff Member.

You may have noticed in the last *Time for action* that as a Staff Member you have a new option to make your group **Publicly Viewable**. This option was not available as a Standard User. Let's have a look at what this means.

Publicly viewable groups

When creating a new group, a Staff Member also gets the option to make a group Publicly Viewable. By setting a group to be Publicly Viewable you are allowing anyone, both within and outside Mahara, to access the group, including any forums that may exist. People outside the site can only **view** the group, not take part in discussions.

As you saw, the option to make your group Publicly Viewable appears on the **Create Group** page when you are setting up your group.

A good example of a time when you might want to make your group Publicly Viewable is when you want users to join your site and take part in discussion. A potential user may find your group via a search engine and discover a forum topic. On realizing that they want to post a response, the user will then need to sign up to join your Mahara. This is great for Mahara sites and groups that reach out into the public domain but is not recommended for those who want their site to be more of a closed "walled garden" for their organization. You should consult with your Site Administrator before making a group open to be publicly viewed to find out if there are any site policies on this.

Now, although Peter Tooley is responsible for the Level 2 NVQ for Mechanical Engineering Course, he isn't the only Assessor of the work that gets submitted. Learner Assessment is also undertaken by one of his colleagues, Susan O'Leary.

Peter would like to allow Susan to use the course group he has just created in order to assess the work of the learners without having to let her use his own login details. But, Peter doesn't want Susan to have any administrative rights over the group. He just needs her to have the ability to see the views that have been submitted in order for her to assess and give feedback upon the work that has been submitted by her learners.

Luckily, Mahara can make this possible with the role known as a group **Tutor**.

Tutors

Tutors can only be set up within a course group; it is not a site-wide role. A Tutor within a controlled group has the ability to view all the work that has been submitted there for assessment. They are also able to release the work back to the learner once it has been assessed. They don't, however, have the ability to manage the group users or forums in the same way that the group administrator is able to.

Let's set up our very first Tutor in our course group. We will set up Susan O'Leary in the NVQ Level 2 course group as an example.

Time for action – adding a Tutor to your course group

1. Log into your Mahara as the same Staff Member as in the previous *Time for action*. The course group you created should still be there.

2. Search for a user in your site that you would like to make a Tutor in your course group. Click on the user to access their profile.

3. Then, from their profile page, add them to your course group by selecting the appropriate course from the **Add to** drop-down box. Then click on **Add.**

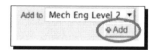

4. Navigate to your course group using either the **Groups | My Groups** menu options, or more quickly by clicking on the group in the groups list to the right of your home screen (Again, revisit Chapter 5 if you are having trouble locating your group).

5. Click on the **Members** tab of your group. In there you should see the user whom you have added in step 3. Peter Tooley of Training 4 Work has identified Susan O'Leary as a Tutor of his NVQ Level 2 group.

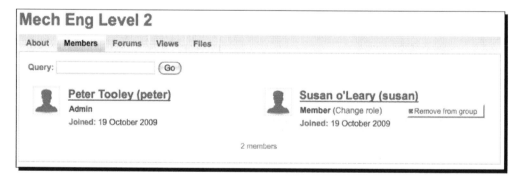

6. Currently, you should see that your user is set as a **Member** of the group. We want them to be a "Tutor". Click on the **Change role** link next to the text saying "Member".

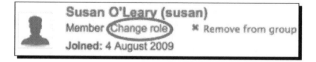

7. You will now see a screen that invites you to change the role of the user. Currently their role is set as Member. Use the drop-down box to the right of the text saying **Change role to** and select **Tutor** from the available options.

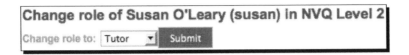

8. To finish, click **Submit**.

That's it! You have a Tutor in your course group. You should see that your users' details have now changed from being a Member, to being a **Tutor** in the description next to their name:

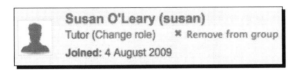

What just happened?

We have just learned how to create a Tutor within a course group.

Susan O'Leary has become a Tutor because she needs to assess work submitted by learners as evidence of their competencies for an engineering qualification. There are other reasons why we might set up Tutors, though. Punam from Pennytown Primary might set up some of her teaching assistants as Tutors in order that they too can give feedback on work that gets submitted during their course. Staff members in PI Inc might use Tutors in course groups when, for example, they want to validate and approve information submitted about pharmaceutical processes before it is published to the site.

Human Resources Managers might use Mahara for monthly **CPD (Continuous Professional Development)** reports and a departmental director might use the Tutor role to delegate supervisory responsibilities to departmental subordinates.

Back to Susan O'Leary from Training 4 Work, who would like to know exactly what process her learners have to go through to submit work to her.

Have a go hero – set up some course groups

Think about some of the courses that you currently run offline in your institution. Could your learners create some views that can be submitted to you for assessment? Create some course groups for those courses and set up some Tutors who will be helping you to manage and assess the work that is submitted to you.

Submitting work for assessment

When used as a learning environment, any assessment process conducted within Mahara shouldn't sacrifice its learner-driven principles. The way that Mahara has set up course groups allows this to be the case. It is the learners themselves who get to choose exactly what work they submit and exactly when they submit that work. This, we believe, is the way things should be.

Let's now find out what a learner has to do to submit a view for assessment by a Tutor or Administrator in a controlled group.

Time for action – submitting a view to a course group for assessment

For this *Time for action*, you will need to be logged in as a standard user who has been added to your course group. Add a standard member to your group if none already exist. As Group Administrator, Peter Tooley of Training 4 Work has added one learner who he knows will be taking his NVQ Level 2 course called Ravinda Pavel. We will be using Ravinda as an example here.

1. Log in to your Mahara as a standard course member belonging to the course group you created earlier.

2. Using everything you learned in Chapters 2 and 4, create a view that you think would be of a good quality to submit to your group for assessment. Save your view when you are happy with it. Ravinda has created this view to submit for assessment:

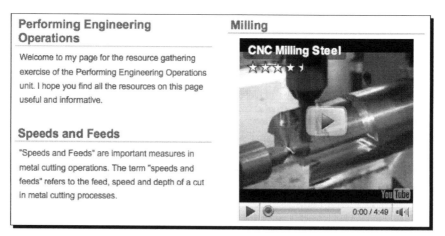

3. Find the view that you created in step 2 in the **My Views** section of **My Portfolio**.

4. Where it says **Submit this View to** select the appropriate course group from the drop-down list. It is likely that you only have one course group to submit to at the moment but in the future you might belong to more than one course and want to select a specific group to submit to. Ravinda is going to submit his view to the NVQ Level 2 group, so he selects **NVQ Level 2** from the drop-down:

5. Click **Submit**. When you have submitted your view, you will see a box explaining that your view won't be editable until your Tutor has finished marking it; just click **Yes** to finish.

What just happened?

We have just seen how easy it is for a learner to submit work to their Tutor using course groups.

We suggested that the view, once it has been sent and is in the hands of the tutor/assessor cannot be edited by the learner. This is true in the sense that the learner cannot access their view to edit and move their blocks around, but they can still view it and edit their access rights.

However, we need to make clear at this point that the view that a Tutor sees may still not be displaying *exactly* the same content that the user saw when they submitted it.

The reason for this potential variation is because the view may contain content that is being linked to, or updated. For example, if a learner has added a blog listing or an RSS feed to their view, it is likely that they have added to their blog since submitting. In this situation the blog postings in the view will also update and be different to those that were originally there at the time of submission. Similarly, any externally linked websites may be displaying different text/video at the time of assessment to those they were displaying at the point of submission. Therefore, it is important that you, as a Tutor, are aware that the submitted view isn't necessarily completely static.

With that qualifier acknowledged, view submission is clearly a great assessment technique for a Tutor. The Tutor knows that the user cannot edit the view in any way other than in the ways we just discussed. This gives them time to look at the view and to grade or assess it. When the Tutor has come up with a decision about what mark it should get, they are then able to release the view back to the learner – leaving the learner free again to edit, extend, and reuse this work in the future.

Copy your view before submitting.

Once you have submitted your view to a course group for assessment you cannot access it for further editing. Therefore, it is a good idea to copy your view before you submit it. This way you can access your work and edit it if you want to whilst your other "copy" is still locked for assessment.

So, we've seen how to submit a view. Now, let's find out how a view is returned to a learner once it has been assessed...

Time for action – releasing a view submitted for assessment

1. Log into Mahara as either a Tutor or Administrator of the course group you have created.

2. Navigate to your course group.

3. The first thing you should notice when you enter your group is that you have a new section at the bottom of the group About page called **views submitted to this group**. In this section you should see all the views that have been submitted here for assessment. Susan O'Leary, our Tutor on the NVQ Level 2 for Mechanical Engineering can now see the work that Ravinda has completed:

> **Views submitted to this group**
>
> PEO: Resource Gathering Exercise by Ravinda Pavel

4. Click on the view that has been submitted for assessment.

5. At this point, imagine yourself in the role of a Tutor. You are able to take your time looking carefully at the submission before giving it a mark, safe in the knowledge that the learner can't make any edits to the view that you can see (apart from the above-mentioned ability to update their blogs, feeds, or external websites).

6. When you are satisfied that you have decided what mark the work deserves you can release it back to the learner. To do this, click on the **Release View** button at the bottom left of the view. Sally O'Leary is happy with her mark for Ravinda Pavel and so she is going to release the view back to him:

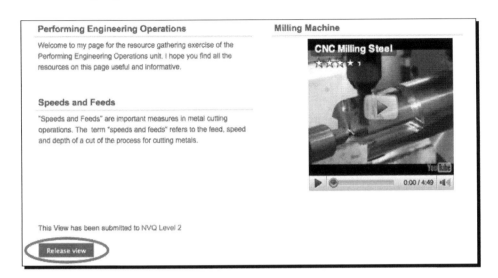

What just happened?

We just found how a Tutor can release a view back to a learner once it has been marked, completing the assessment process.

In Chapter 4 we saw how you can give feedback on views. Use this feature to give your learners constructive advice on what they did/didn't do well when creating their view. It is probably best if you make this feedback private so that only the user can see what you have written.

Putting it all together into an assessment process

So far in this chapter, we have seen how powerful Institutions and Course Groups can be in providing a bit more control for Administrators and Staff in a Mahara Site. We have also seen the basis of a simple Assessment Process based around learners submitting views to a course group. Now, let's combine all that we've seen to create an assessment process in Mahara.

First, we'll hear again from Neil from Training 4 Work:

----- Neil from Training 4 Work thinks -----

It is looking great now that Graham has his own institution. He was telling me how he's used this chapter to set up Peter Tooley as a Staff Member so that he can create a Controlled Group for his NVQ Level 2 course.

Now I know a little bit more, I have had some ideas about what we can do to make the assessment process work better in Mahara. While we want each of our learners to creatively express themselves as individuals when they are submitting their ePortfolios, it will also be useful for us to give them a scaffold upon which to build their content. From our perspective, this will go some way towards ensuring that each learner submits everything they are supposed to. It also provides a starting point for the learner rather than asking them to start from a blank view. To achieve this in Mahara we can use the templating feature I read about earlier in the book. Our staff can create copyable views to give their learners something to start from.

Neil is right, the view templating system in Mahara is a great way of suggesting standard layout for work that is to be submitted by all learners.

Of course, a learner could take the template, change it completely, and then submit that completely new set of information. But, depending on the course, they may then be failed for this level of "creativity". The decision here is up to the assessor concerned. The important thing is that Mahara believes that a modern learner need not sacrifice their right to personalize the presentation of their own content and of their own work, even if it may still remain wise for them to largely follow the conventions suggested by a tutor or a qualification.

Let's now show Mahara in action by devising a full assessment process, including the use of these templates and showing how we can involve people external to the Mahara site (such as somebody verifying the standard of the submitted work for an examining body) in the assessment process. The process described works for the UK-centric NVQ delivery example we are using here, but it is also general enough to apply to any type of qualification that requires evidence or work to be submitted for assessment. We can use Mahara nowadays to submit formally-assessed work digitally in a similar way to the way learners might, in the past, have submitted a paper-based portfolio, poster, or worksheet for assessment.

Time for action – an example assessment process with Mahara

1. As a Staff Member, create a course group.

2. Add all your learners to the group that you just created.

3. In the "Views" section of your course group create a view and make it copyable by checking the **Allow Copying** box in the view settings.

4. Add to the template a basic description of what the learner should be loading into which sections. Here is very simple example of the kind of template you may create:

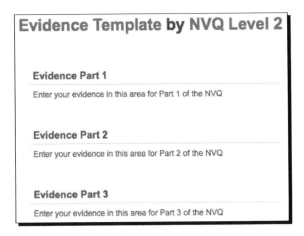

Evidence Template by NVQ Level 2

Evidence Part 1

Enter your evidence in this area for Part 1 of the NVQ

Evidence Part 2

Enter your evidence in this area for Part 2 of the NVQ

Evidence Part 3

Enter your evidence in this area for Part 3 of the NVQ

5. Save your View when you are happy with it. It should now be seen by all your learners in the course group.

6. Encourage your learners to copy the template view to their own portfolio area. Here they can make adjustments to it, adding their own information for assessment.

7. When they are happy with their work, the learners should submit their view back to the group for assessment.

8. You can assess a learner's work, choosing to add feedback to their work if you want them to review it and resubmit it to you.

9. Now, in the files area of the group, you can upload documents and make them only viewable by tutors/administrators. One idea is to share a spreadsheet showing the marks for all of the students at this point showing their progress on the course. This spreadsheet can then be displayed to people verifying quality of the work (either internal or external to the Mahara site). You may also want to put files in the files area to explain a little more about how the learners are going to be assessed and how they submit work for assessment.

10. At this point, the tutors are ready to look at all the work that has been submitted and mark it.

11. Finally, when marks have been decided the views are released back to the learners.

What just happened?

We have just gone through a simple process showing how you could use Mahara templates along with course groups to assess learner evidence.

Monitoring and assessing learners' work

Many Tutors giving feedback on a learner's work like to use the facility Mahara provides to add a file to the feedback they provide. This could be a spreadsheet or word processed document giving feedback according to formalized assessment criteria, for example.

Other tutors like to make use of the "Add to Watchlist" option – where a learner allows a tutor to watch and give feedback on the way the learner is developing their view before it gets formally submitted for assessment. For this to happen, the learner has to share access to their own view by allowing access by their tutor on their view's Access settings. While a learner may want to informally engage a tutor's support in the development of their work in this way, they also retain their right to choose for themselves which of their views the tutor gets to see and which ones they don't.

We suggested earlier in this chapter that you might want to work collaboratively with your tutors to share the results of your assessment. We mentioned that you could share a file in the files area with permissions set so that file isn't editable or readable by standard users (you probably don't want learners seeing the progress of and marks awarded to their colleagues). Another idea is to set up a Google document (spreadsheet or word processed file – see: http://docs.google.com) which contains all the results. Again, permissions settings would be important here and this could be linked to from a private view in the course group or even from the Group's "About" page.

Link to a Moodle course

Do you also run a Moodle installation for your institution/business? Why not put a "new window" link to a related Moodle course page within the description on the About page of your Mahara Course Group? This way, learners can access Moodle course materials whilst working within the Mahara Group. Your Site Administrator could even set this up so that you have single-sign on functionality.

We also mentioned that as part of the process for assessment in Mahara you may want to include people external to the course group or Mahara site to "verify" the quality of work. Here are a couple of ideas for how you could do this:

- **Secret URLs**: Encourage learners to create and send you a Secret URL linking to their views. These links could be collated and sent to an external verifier/marker so that they can see the views.

- Create an **Assessment Page**: The Staff Member for the group (person responsible for assessment) could create a special Assessment View. This view could contain links to all the views that require external review. This page could also contain links to a mark book in a Course Management System, such as Moodle to show results of quizzes that users may have taken alongside creating their Mahara view.

It is important to note in this chapter that, while Mahara has facilitated assessment of learning in this way, Mahara has no intention of ever becoming a Learning Management System. Moodle is a formalized Course and Learning Management System. Mahara isn't. Instead, Mahara is, and will always remain, an informal and personalized learning environment.

One of the very reasons Mahara is so keen on maintaining its symbiotic relationship with Moodle (`http://moodle.org`) is because Mahara sees the benefits of the integration of its own informal learning model with Moodle's Gradebook facility. Informal learning might ultimately get submitted for formal assessment in an online course just as easily as it can be submitted for assessment in an offline course (as we have described in this chapter).

Useful notes on Moodle and Mahara Integration (creating what the community have affectionately named a "Mahoodle" environment) can be accessed via the Mahara Wiki: `http://wiki.mahara.org/System_Administrator%27s_Guide/Moodle%2f%2fMahara_Integration`.

We think it is also worth pointing out at the close of this chapter the extremely useful work that has been done by the lead Mahara partner in the UK, the University of London Computer Centre (ULCC). In a highly pedagogically sound quest to promote and facilitate the delivery of personalized learning, the ULCC have developed their "Personalization of Learning Framework":

`http://moodle.ulcc.ac.uk/course/view.php?id=139`

This framework elegantly integrates Mahara (as a Personal Learning Space) and Moodle (as a Virtual Learning Environment) together with two open source Moodle Modules, which ULCC have written themselves:

Assessment Manager for progress tracking and verification evidence towards formally accredited qualification (which is a significant improvement on the spreadsheet in the course group files area or the Google Doc we mentioned earlier in this chapter): `http://moodle.ulcc.ac.uk/course/view.php?id=140`.

ULCC ILP for facilitating tutor support including target setting and progress reviews: `http://moodle.ulcc.ac.uk/course/view.php?id=107`. It is worth pointing out here that this ILP Module can be configured to "listen to" data sent to it from many of the popular Management Information Systems used by schools, colleges, universities, and other training providers.

Most Mahara partners can host all of the above extensions to Mahara for you, if you are interested, but there will, obviously, be an extra cost to the hosting and support.

There has also been some work done to integrate Mahara with Website Content Management Systems such as Drupal: `http://drupal.org`.

Pop quiz – Course Groups, Staff Members and Tutors

- What is possible with a Course Group that isn't with a standard group?
- What is a Staff Member able to do that standard users can't?
- What can a Tutor do?

Summary

In this chapter we gave you a sneak look at administration by showing you a bit of what an Institutional Administrator can do. We also looked at Mahara from a tutor's/staff member's point of view, showing and illustrating what these roles are able to do differently to a standard Mahara member. This allowed us to see how Mahara can be used to develop an assessment process, with views being submitted to tutors for marking. We learned about managing our members as an Institutional Administrator, discovered what a Course Group is and learned how a Course Group differs from a Standard Group. We started to explore the roles and responsibilities of Tutors, worked through the process of submitting work for assessment and releasing it back to a student, and introduced some ideas for how you can use all of these features to develop an assessment process in Mahara.

While we saw that Mahara can be used to assess and give feedback on learners' work with our "tutors' hats on", we pointed out that Mahara is, in itself, making no attempt to become a formalized Learning Management System. Mahara is happier, instead, to work in symbiosis with Moodle or the ULCC Personalization Framework for this more formal type of gradebook-centred progress tracking.

Our book has tried to introduce you to the key aspects involved with being a Mahara site user. We have *not* been trying to teach you the more technical knowledge involved with becoming a Mahara Site Administrator. You may be interested in administering a Mahara site for yourself, however, so we have provided two appendices to help get you started along this journey.

Let's move on now to the appendices, then, where we will begin to get an initial feel of what is involved with being a top-level Mahara Site Administrator.

Mahara Implementation Pre-Planner

In this Appendix, we have laid out and sequenced some of the important questions your organization will need to address if you want to get your ePortfolio system setup quickly, and for it to be a success. This Appendix serves as a Pre-Planner, not as a Planner. It is intended to get you thinking through some of the important issues behind organizational ePortfolio platform implementation. After you have worked through this Appendix, you should then go on to draw up an Implementation Action Plan.

One approach for an Action Plan format that you could draw up, for example, could be based upon the following design:

Mahara Implementation Planner					
Overall Aim:					
PHASE ONE: Analysis and Specification					
Objective 1:					
Action	**Who?**	**By when?**	**Resources required:**	**Planned outcomes and outputs**	**Impact measures**
Objective 2:					
Action	**Who?**	**By when?**	**Resources required:**	**Planned outcomes and outputs**	**Impact measures**

PHASE TWO: Design and Implementation					
Objective 1:					
Action	**Who?**	**By when?**	**Resources required:**	**Planned outcomes and outputs**	**Impact measures**
Objective 2:					
Action	**Who?**	**By when?**	**Resources required:**	**Planned outcomes and outputs**	**Impact measures**
PHASE THREE: Evaluation and Continuation					
Objective 1:					
Action	**Who?**	**By when?**	**Resources required:**	**Planned outcomes and outputs**	**Impact measures**
Objective 2:					
Action	**Who?**	**By when?**	**Resources required:**	**Planned outcomes and outputs**	**Impact measures**

Here a matrix table should be added as appended with the mail. Please let me know when you reach here. A `.odt` *and also a* `.doc` *version of the above matrix is available for download from* `http://maharaforbeginners.tdm.info`.

It is our hope that by getting you to think through the questions below, we will help you to avoid a failed software implementation. Successful software implementations have more to do with cultural changes than they have to do with technological changes. Too many software implementations have failed and so, let's make sure, if we can, that yours is not one of those failures. A classic failed software implementation runs like this:

- One management member opts to adopt while others look skeptically on

- The manager brings in designers to install, configure, and launch the software

- Staff and user time is not provided, neither is any further training, guidance, and development time planned or purchased

- The implementation quickly starts to lose direction and the project fails

Let's be clear again, this Mahara Implementation Pre-Planner will only serve to guide your decision-making process; we cannot make your decisions for you and we are leaving it up to you to form your formal implementation strategy for yourself.

Please bear in mind also that as we write this Implementation Pre-Planner, we are catering for a wide readership, so some of the questions and suggestions we make below might sometimes be pitched at a larger, or smaller, or just a different organization to your own, and they may not all always seem relevant to your context. If this is the case, just skip that question or suggestion and move on to the next one.

You need to start thinking about what you will need to do and what your people will need to happen if you are going to make it happen.

So, now that all of our disclaimers are out of the way, please read on.

What's involved with a Mahara implementation?

Although real life is not always as neat and tidy as we would like it to be, a Mahara implementation will essentially pass through three broadly distinct stages:

1. Analysis and Specification
2. Design and Implementation
3. Evaluation and Continuation

To scaffold your Mahara implementation here, we have decided to take you through a sequence of opinions, questions, and suggestions. We have split those broader stages into some smaller phases as follows:

ANALYSIS AND SPECIFICATION

Phase 1: Decide if Mahara is right for you.

Phase 2: Understand your own specific needs and working conditions.

Phase 3: Choose between a Mahara-partner supported site or your own installation.

Phase 4: Scope out your implementation plan.

DESIGN AND IMPLEMENTATION

Phase 5: Create a Buzz!

Phase 6: Get some quick wins in first!

Phase 7: Continuously involve the users in your design process.

Phase 8: Keep going despite adversity!

EVALUATION AND CONTINUATION

Phase 9: Review and Re-evaluate.

Phase 10: Change and Embed.

Analysis and Specification

Certainly, the most important phase of all to get the correct result is the Analysis and Specification phase. It is always best to try your absolute hardest to iron out as many difficulties as you can before you unleash any new learning process upon your end users.

Deciding if Mahara is right for you

Before you do anything else, consider why you want a lifelong learning ePortfolio system such as Mahara, and whether you have the appropriate working conditions to make it successful. There are, broadly speaking, two different types of ePortfolio system. The institutionally owned learning management system and the learner-owned lifelong learning system.

As we have demonstrated in this book, Mahara is very much the latter. Mahara is focused on offering learners a place to gather, store, and share their work with others as they progress along their personal, lifelong learning journeys.

Some other ePortfolio systems are focused, instead, on offering a facility to track learner-submitted work according to institutional—or accrediting body—needs. That is not what Mahara is about.

Mahara is a user-centred informal, reflective learning environment, which also:

◆ Provides a system for uploading and getting feedback on assessment items.

◆ Facilitates social networking in "Communities of Practice".

◆ Provides a platform from which a user can present their learning and competencies to others, for example a prospective employer, an application to a university, a promotion panel, or during a professional development review.

- Supports a simple personal and professional development planning process helping a learner with their action planning for their lifelong learning or career development processes.

- Supports platform integration with an ever expanding range of Web 2.0 tools such as YouTube and Picasa.

- Provides a templating facility for ePortfolio pages.

- Acts as a walled garden where you control the user base.

- Provides a very private individual storage space for a learner's own artefacts.

- Allows for individual and collaborative group Views (Views is the Mahara word for Web Pages).

- Offers ease of use (no need to be a webhead!).

- Offers monitoring of other people's Views by means of a watchlist.

- Allows you to give feedback on other people's Views.

- Allows for moderation where you can check before a View goes public.

- Allows you to limit and extend users' storage space.

- Runs on a web server (making it available whenever and from wherever).

- Offers the option to copy and move your portfolio to another location (including non-Mahara ePortfolio applications that support LEAP2A).

Mahara itself is NOT a Learning Management System. It therefore does not:

- Cross-reference against assessment/accreditation criteria set out by an accrediting body (such as formative and summative assessment trackers, or occupational standards for NVQs in the UK).

- Provide an audit trail of submitted and graded work.

- Neatly archive and retain learner submitted work.

Mahara does, however, understand and respond to the fact that some institutions like to formally assess their learners' work while still adopting a personalized learning approach as their driving paradigm. One option a learner may have in Mahara is to submit their work for assessment by tutors (see Chapter 7). However, the tracking of learner progress would then have to be facilitated by integrating Mahara with another system such as:

- A tutor maintained spreadsheet. This could be stored and shared in a Mahara group files area or a within a Google document for example.

- A spreadsheet on Google Docs.

- The Gradebook in Moodle (`http://wiki.mahara.org/Roadmap/Moodle_Mahara_Integration`). Mahara already supports Single-Sign-On integration with Moodle, a system that can be used for assessment of achievements according to some criteria. This can be used to track progress against a time-tabled program of activity.

- The ULCC Assessment Manager Module for Moodle (`http://moodle.ulcc.ac.uk/course/view.php?id=140`). This assessment manager module is a highly sophisticated learner progress tracking module, which can be used for a wide range of qualifications, both inside and outside the UK.

Mahara itself, then, is not trying to be a Learning Management System. It is a place where learners can reflect on their learning and showcase their work to others.

The view of the Mahara project is that Moodle (and its competitor LMSs/VLEs) should do Moodle-like things and Mahara should do Mahara-like things. From Moodle V2.0 onwards, Moodle will provide a portfolio API, which will allow single click export of files uploaded into Moodle across as artefacts in your own Mahara space. There is a plan to make it so that Mahara Views can be submitted as "assignments" in Moodle and thereby, graded and tracked within the Moodle gradebook. All of this will enable learners to use Moodle for "taught", "outcomes-driven", assessment processes and Mahara for their more personalized, and more ongoing, reflection/informal learning activities.

If you have decided that a lifelong learning ePortfolio like Mahara is for you, it is now wise to decide properly whether or not Mahara is actually the platform that is best-suited for your organizational needs.

> *Danube University (Austria) researchers, Himpsl and Baumgartner, published their Evaluation of ePortfolio Software in February 2009 (download the PDF at* `http://epac.pbworks.com/f/ijet_paper_himpsl_baumgartner.pdf`*).*

Himpsl and Baumgartner evaluated and compared a range of lifelong learning ePortfolio solutions against the following criteria (and subcriteria):

- Input of keywords
- Internal cross-references
- External cross-references
- Publication on the web
- Pricing and license schemes
- Simple data export
- Support of all currently used A-grade browsers

Collecting, organizing, selecting

- Simple data import
- Comfortable data import
- Searching, sequencing, and filtering
- Annotations to files
- Aggregating (integration of external data via feeds)
- Version control of files

Reflecting, testing, verifying, and planning

- Guidelines for reflection
- Guidelines for competences
- Guidelines for evaluation (self assessment, assessment by others)
- Guidelines for goals, personal development, and career management
- Guidelines for feedback (advice, tutoring, mentoring)

Representing and publishing

- Access control by users (owner, peers, authority, public)
- Adaptation of the display: layout (flexible placing, boilerplates)
- Adaptation of the display: colors, fonts, design
- Publishing of several portfolios, or alternatively, various views

Administrating, implementing, adapting

- Development potential of the provider, company profile
- Enabling technologies (programming language, operating system, and so on)
- Authentication and user administration (backed-up interfaces, and so on)
- e-Learning standards
- Migration/storage/export

Usability

- User interface
- Syndicating (choice of feeds for the individual portfolio)
- Availability, accessibility
- Navigation/initial training/help
- External and internal information function
- Interchangeable, adaptable user-defined boilerplates
- Personal storage, respectively export function

As you can probably guess, Mahara does very well in this comparison. It comes out joint-top of the list alongside a proprietary (and equally excellent, if very different) alternative ePortfolio solution known as PebblePad (http://www.pebblepad.co.uk/).

PebblePad, as good as it is, is not open-source though. The fact that Mahara is an open-source and modular product means that:

- The code may be copyrighted by others (mostly by Catalyst IT) but it is under an open license, meaning that it will always be available for all of us to use, and that it will always be cost-free for us to reuse

- You can, therefore, switch your technical support agency at any point (there is no vendor lock-in)

- The product will always exist even if the current maintainers (currently Catalyst IT in New Zealand) choose to discontinue their support for it

- Everybody can collaborate to develop what we need (there is a modular/plugin architecture)

Understanding your own specific needs and working conditions

Never look for some place new to go until you completely understand and appreciate where you already are. Never try to make a change until you have a clear vision, and understand fully the benefits you will gain from making that change.

Here's how to start!

1. Clearly set out your overall aims:

    - What business objectives need to be achieved?

    - What organizational objectives need to be achieved?

    - What educational objectives need to be achieved?

2. Understand your own working context: If you find yourself answering *no* to any of the questions below. You should start thinking "Is it actually possible to turn this *no* into a *yes*?"

    i. Do all of your stakeholders: your leaders, teacher/tutors, day-to-day administrators, IT support staff, and your future end users all have a common vision for your ePortfolio? (Even if you are working as a go-it-alone teacher, are you sure enough of your students will buy this?)

    ii. Is there a **supportive external context** for your ePortfolio implementation? Is there explicit support for this coming to you, for example, from central office, from government-funded agencies, or from accrediting bodies, trade guilds or worker's unions?

iii. Is there, and will there be, a **consistent** and **reliable** inflow of funding for your site's support?

iv. Will there be a dedicated **steering group** of visionaries and power-brokers who will work to make your implementation a success?

v. Will you **continuously** invest to employ or upskill the **competent staff** you will need in order to disseminate knowledge to newer users?

3. Ensure you have a sufficiently skilled and available (time/motivation to support?) technical and pedagogical support infrastructures in place.

4. Ensure that your target end users have appropriate access to your Mahara system in terms not only of a reasonable internet supply, but also in terms of physical access to machines in both working and home-life contexts.

5. Understand that change affects emotions:

Successful change = Vision + Skills + Incentives + Resources + Action Plan

If you are going to successfully implement an ePortfolio solution, you need to be able to develop and disseminate a shared vision. This vision optimistically encourage people to embrace changes in both technology-adoption and learning approaches. To succeed, this needs top-level support and needs to be a fully aligned part of a whole organizational approach. You will not only need to model the way for others to follow, you will also need to enable and to motivate others to act.

You will need to know and to broadcast to your people where you are going, and why you are going that way. You will need to put the required training in place to make that vision happen. People will need incentives. Incentives can be financial, recognition-oriented, status-oriented, promotion-oriented, and so forth. Adoption of your new ePortfolio system should probably become an expectation, part of a learner's assessment criteria, part of a tutor's job description. You will also need a clearly structured action plan, appropriately designated responsibilities alongside sensible timescales.

The next table from Thousand, R and Villa, J neatly illustrates the negative emotional impact likely to arise (notice in particular the far right-hand column), if just one of these elements is not in place.

Complex change and emotional impact table (Source: *Thousand, R and Villa, J. [2001]. Managing Complex Change*):

Vision	Skills	Incentives	Resources	Action Plan	Results in
a	a	a	a	a	Change
–	a	a	a	a	Confusion
a	–	a	a	a	Anxiety
a	a	–	a	a	Opposition
a	a	a	–	a	Frustration
a	a	a	a	–	False starts

Prof. Gordon Joyes from the University of Nottingham first introduced us to the "Threshold Concepts" and to their importance when applied to an ePortfolio implementation. Joyes attributes the idea of Threshold Concepts to Jan Meyer and Ray Land (`http://www.etl. tla.ed.ac.uk//docs/ETLreport4.pdf`). Essentially, the point being made is that in order for somebody to perform a task effectively, they need to go through some "doorways" of understanding. If these doorway "thresholds" are not traversed, the activity is not likely to be a success. For those of us implementing ePortfolios and encouraging their adoption, Joyes and his colleagues have so far come up with five important threshold concepts:

Concept 1: Purpose

The PURPOSE(S) for the ePortfolio must be aligned to the particular context. You need to make your ePortfolio genuinely work for you. It should help you to perform your learning and business functions effectively.

Concept 2: Learning Activity Design

There must be a conscious DESIGN & SUPPORT OF A LEARNING ACTIVITY/ACTIVITIES suited to the purpose and the context. Mahara alone is nothing without a clear organizational sense of learning delivery structure. Your tutors need to be adopting a learner-driven, personalized learning delivery model, only then will Mahara be able to come into its own as a useful resource.

Concept 3: Processes

The PROCESSES involved in the creation of the ePortfolio in this context must be understood and both technical and pedagogic support needs to be provided. Both staff and learners need to be trained to understand how the platform works, and also how it can be made to work to best effect.

Concept 4: Ownership

ePortfolio processes and outcomes need to be OWNED by the student. This not only leads to considering portability of their data but also to whether the tool allows the use of their own phone camera, audio recorder, Web 2.0 applications, and so on. It also leads us to consider the learners' genuine engagement with our Mahara platform. The learners need to see the Mahara environment as their own. They need to see it as a useful resource, which helps them to engage with your institution as they learn.

Concept 5: Disruptive Nature

ePortfolios are DISRUPTIVE from a pedagogic, technological, and an organizational perspective. It is unlikely that Mahara will fit exactly within existing system. Some changes will need to be made, and this will upset some people and disrupt some existing processes.

Unless we understand these five (and probably) more issues, we won't succeed in our action plan. By understand, I mean more than simply *know* that they are issues. We don't just need to be aware of these issues but also, actually need to understand at our very core that these are centrally important—indeed key—to the success of our ePortfolio implementation. Unless we are practically oriented towards implementing our ePortfolios while taking these issues into account, we must truly understand that we are likely to struggle.

Choosing between a Mahara partner-supported site or your own installation

The trade-off is usually the extent and expertise of the support available (for example, from a Mahara partner) versus the amount of control you have over your own system (for example, total control over your own server). A compromise is usually possible and most Mahara partners are willing to serve to support your managers, educators, and IT experts to support themselves. A full list of official Mahara partners can be viewed at `http://mahara.org/partners`.

Scoping out your implementation plan

You are going to have to draw up some sort of implementation plan. We will leave you to determine for yourself how best to draw this up, but we will raise here some of the issues we think you will need to address. Essentially, you are going to have to manage five actions:

1. Decide on your implementation timeframe.
2. Ensure you have the people's commitment.
3. Draft out your initial Mahara design.
4. Draft out your Mahara-specific policies.
5. Start to embed Mahara usage into wider institutional and program priorities (more on this later).

Decide on your implementation timeframe

Your implementation timeframe may be longer or shorter depending upon factors such as:

◆ The size of your organization. (Are you going to implement at local level or at a large scale?)

◆ The complexity of the Mahara platform you decide to implement.

◆ The levels of digital literacy amongst your client group. (Does your action team or do your consultants have the expertise and motivation to develop significant content quickly?) You will probably need, after all, to structure your site as well as to model the way in terms of profile page and view-creation. (Do your end users suffer much from tech-fear?) As well as providing Mahara training, there may be a local need for you to focus on more basic digital literacies (how to record audio, how to plugin a webcam, how to transfer an image from a digital camera, knowledge of data formats such as `.pdf` versus `.doc` and `.odt`, `.avi` or `.mp4` versus `.flv`, and so on).

◆ What staff resources you have available. (Are you directing staff or temporary consultants according to a project implementation plan? Are you allowing these people the time they will really need? Alternatively, are you happy for a much slower and more participative development process?).

Ensure you have the people's commitment

In a large organizational implementation, if the ePortfolio idea does not have the support of 75% of the organization's senior management team, it is unlikely to be a success. Your leadership has to be dedicated to committing both financial and staffing resources to the implementation project! You will need to set up a *steering group* if you really want the implementation to happen and this steering group will have to include at least one major power-broker from your organization and at least one Mahara expert or visionary. Again, you may be wise to bring in a Mahara partner consultant as your expert/visionary.

In a smaller, more local implementation, the potential users really need to be telling you that they like the idea of using a digital ePortfolio before you throw yourself into it. Bear in mind that people often dislike *anything* they don't already know.

Draft out your initial Mahara design

◆ Make sure you have a good understanding of how Mahara works before you start. You have already made a good start by buying and reading this book. While it is wise to be aware of the fact that your Mahara design may well change significantly as time goes on, it is even wiser to have a clear understanding of how your site is going to be essentially structured right from the onset. Let's get thinking! Who is going to design and set up your Mahara site? Are you giving them the time they need to do it?

- What are you going to do in terms of site theming?

- Are you going to reconfigure your Mahara site to work differently in any way? If so, you might have to buy in the right expertise to achieve this. One of the benefits of open source software is precisely its configurability, but you will still need to buy in the skills to make these configurations happen. You may wish to integrate your Mahara look, feel, and functionality with your Moodle site for example, or with a website Content Management System such as Joomla. Alternatively, you may wish to change aspects of the Mahara code to make it work in a particular way you want it to work. Some organizations, for example, like to change the word "Resumé" to "CV", others like, for example, to close off the "friends" functionality within their site.

- Are there any integrations with other software that you will need to set up (such as Moodle)?

- Who will be the site administrator: controlling users, checking storage limits, monitoring acceptable use, and so forth? If a staff member, will this be a dedicated element of their job description? Could you outsource this type of administrative support to, for example, a Mahara partner?

- Who will be responsible for monitoring external software developments, interoperability developments, and so on?

- Who is going to administer and report back on any end-user surveys you conduct?

- Who is going to be your pedagogical visionary? How much time (and remuneration) are they going to get to give presentations and enthuse about online reflective learning and knowledge transfer?

- Will you give any paid time to the tutors or managers you will be expecting to "lead the way" with your ePortfolio system? Will work on the ePortfolio platform become a paid element of their work, clearly articulated within their job description and properly timetabled into their working week?

- Will your IT support staff need Mahara training? Who will run this training?

- Who will provide the first line technical support? (Basic help such as: "How do I log in?", "How do I upload my file?") Would you prefer to outsource this support? Could you arrange and publish a timetable of offline and/or telephone and/or internet-live-support-based Mahara user "Support Surgeries" in which less competent users could approach competent ones for friendly and informal advice and support?

- Who will provide higher-level technical support into the long-term? For example, bug fixing, updating, upgrading, integrating (with other software), modifying, or extending your platform according to your needs. Would this be cheap and safe to outsource (an outsource supplier is often less likely to leave you in the lurch than would be an employee)?

- What Mahara user institutions are you going to set up, if any?
- What will be your core Mahara groups? Who should set these up?
- What will those groups actually exist to do? What will be their purpose?

 Start off by describing what already happens in a particular focus area offline and then apply that to what you hope will happen online.

- Who will be allocated responsibility for encouraging and moderating activity in those groups?
- What Views will need to be produced for your site?
- What other sites will need to link across to your Mahara site?
- What will be the main weblinks you will need to link to from your site?
- Who will set and monitor performance targets? Will this be a part of their job description?

Draft out your Mahara-specific policies

You need to be crystal clear about the rules of engagement! It is only fair on your end users and it is also fair on you. There is also, very often, an organizational need to draw up and adhere to formal policies. Here are some thoughts in this respect:

- What promises can you make: the provision of internet access? Will it be always available, freely available, and maintain a reasonable level of quality/stability?
- What terms and conditions of use will you need the users to agree to?
- Is it important to set out an acceptable use policy?
- What privacy rights does the user have?
- Does the user leave their data with you when they complete their course/program/ employment period? If so, for how long will they have access to the data they leave?
- We advise you to leave intellectual property in the hands of the ePortfolio users themselves and not in the hands of your institution. ePortfolios should (in our view) be owned by the users themselves and remain their own responsibility until they contravene the institution's terms and conditions of acceptable use. This is often not possible, though. In the case of schools, colleges, and polytechnics, some countries make the institutions responsible (by law) to guarantee that no inappropriate content is hosted on their servers. If this is your case, you may have decide to set up a procedure for regular spot-checks where an administrator masquerades as a random sample of learners (for instance, each month) to check up on users within your system.

◆ How effectively are you going to communicate policies such as these to your end users?

Start to embed Mahara into institutional and program priorities

If yours is a small-scale implementation, might you just be trailblazing the way for a large-scale implementation across your whole organization? If so, or if you are a larger organization already, here are some questions to get you thinking:

◆ Is Mahara usage a stated element of your curriculum delivery? Is it the time to learn how to use Mahara explicitly allocated as part of a new user's workload?

◆ Is any requirement to engage with Mahara in a course, job role, or program clearly communicated and understood well in advance of any requirement to submit work?

◆ Is Mahara usage referred to in your business development plan, organizational plan, and job description?

◆ Is Mahara utilized in your *quality improvement* reviews and processes?

◆ Is Mahara adoption and use measured in your q*uality improvement* reviews and processes?

◆ Are Mahara development workshops a fixed element of your staff's Induction and Continuous Professional Development Plans? Staff should be regularly discussing not only how to use the system technically, but also how to use the system for best learning and business impact and effect!

Design and implementation

Once you have thoughtfully made the decision, set up the guiding team, and scope out the plan for a Mahara implementation, you will need to get into the nitty-gritty of making it happen.

Creating a buzz!

Whether you are running a large-scale implementation or a small-scale local implementation, you are going to have to motivate and enable your end users to engage. Here are some ideas that may help:

◆ Draw up and implement a communications plan that targets all different types of stakeholders, for example users, staff, leaders, trainers, assessors, parents, employers, external agencies, press and media, and so on.

◆ Publicize some real-life case studies and examples of Mahara in action.

- Make sure everyone gets a copy of your new user guide. You could use this book for your staff members and provide or adapt the shorter, simpler guide linked to from the Mahara demo site (`http://demo.mahara.org`) for end users.

- Set the expectations. You may wish to set explicit incentives and penalties connected to user adoption? For instance, If you do X, you get Y... Hurrah!!! If you fail to complete X, Y is the consequence, booooo!!!

- Practically help people to overcome barriers:

    ❏ Share information, using local Wi-Fi hotspots

    ❏ Distribute price comparisons for broadband and 3G

    ❏ Offer support via telephone, face-to-face, live website support or you could set up a Mahara Group as a Helpdesk for your users make sure everyone knows how to access this sort of technical support and advice as and when they need it

- Set up a "User Suggestions" facility, where users can come up with ideas and actively influence what gets practically done with your Mahara.

- Set the standards. One idea is to award "medals" for standards in Views and groups.

Getting some quick wins in first!

While it is crucial that you can see the big picture of what your ePortfolio platform will deliver before you start, it is important not to get bogged down into a big picture and to focus in on some practical deliverables which you can implement quickly. Either you, your platform designer, or your design team will need to quickly implement and equally quickly and publicly celebrate some "quick wins". Let's get you thinking.

- Can you identify some instant fixes where using Mahara would solve a real problem you are facing?

- Alternatively, can you identify which of your own user groups would respond best to—and therefore quickly adopt—a digital ePortfolio as a medium for learning delivery?

- Another thought! If people need to migrate to Mahara from another means of gathering and presenting their ePortfolio evidence (paper-based work, another platform, a USB stick, a wiki, a website, and so on), how are you going to convince them that it will be worth the effort? (Don't forget they can always link back from their new Mahara views to any previous websites they created.)

Continuously involving your users in the design process

You are going to have to ask, listen to, and respond to whatever people want to do in their Mahara! To make your implementation work, you will need to:

1. Conduct regular response analyses.

2. Get together for strategy reviews.

3. Do something in response to what you find out.

You will need to get your people expressing and sharing their ideas, their reflections, and their learning (their Views) within groups of people who share similar interest areas. If you are going to get your Mahara site running you will have to jump on any chance to ignite the fire that will turn it into a lively online community—always dealing with educationally and topically-burning issues of the day as they arise.

Response analyses can be, but need not be dull online or offline survey feedback routines. An equally good response analysis is a show of hands in a meeting, or a chat in a cafeteria.

Further, don't just ask questions like:

◆ Have you used it? How often?

◆ Did you like it? How much?

Also ask more open, forward looking questions like:

◆ How else could using a digital portfolio help you in your life or study?

◆ What other topics would you like to reflect upon with other people?

The most important thing, though, is that you get together to talk about the response and thereby, start to responsively and appropriately review your ongoing strategy.

Remember, a proper Mahara site isn't a miracle of people, it is a miracle of community.

Keep going despite adversity!

Your Mahara implementation process will inevitably meet people who act as "implementation resisters". It is a fact of life that many people react badly to change, even when it is good for them.

You will, therefore, need to apply some "situational response tactics" as your implementation progresses.

People can be implementation resisters

- The Pessimist may say: "We can't change! We're doomed!"

- The Pragmatist may say: "We've done enough, let's not change too far!"

- The Technophobe may say: "This is too difficult for me, it's not fair!"

- The Traditionalist may say: "I'm just too busy for this, this is a nice-to-do, not a have-to-do!"

- The Cynic may say: "This is just a passing fad, ignore it, it will go away!", the Implementation Team's worst enemy...?

- The Critic may say: "Rise up and rebel! We cannot allow this to happen!"

Situational Response Tactics

How will you buy people in? We can apply two types of tactics when we need to subdue the implementation resisters out there: "Big Bombs" and "Sniper Fire".

Situational Response Tactic 1: Big Bombs

We use these tactics to try to affect the feelings of as many people as possible with the least amount of effort. Examples include:

- **Powerbroker support**: Get an institutional authority figure to express support in a public meeting or in a public newsletter.

- **Identify and provide missing information**: Is there something people need to know about Mahara's usefulness that you haven't told them? One example is that Mahara can serve as an online file storage area—a USB stick on the Internet. While this is not what Mahara is actually for, it is a useful utility, which may start getting people to engage.

- **Visiting expert**: Bring in an external speaker, who can talk with expertise about Mahara and ePortfolios.

- **Generic questionnaires**: It is often a good idea to conduct a feedback survey, which picks up the mood of the crowd. The magic here lies in the public report-back stage in which you state what the crowd responded and go on to carefully and usefully explain where and why you agree and disagree.

- **User guide promotions**: Run events to promote your new user guides. Give out user guides at parties, in group meetings and events, in cafes, in induction programs, during training events, and so on.

- **Poster campaign**: Display posters all around your institution promoting use of your ePortfolio. For example, the Mahara logo with "Mahara means thinking" or "Mahara makes ME think!" written on it. (You may of course have a different institutional name for your own Mahara install and so will come up with better, more localized, poster ideas.)

- **Competitions and celebrations**: Best View awards, most "medals" awards (as discussed previously), busiest user awards, most innovative online thought of the year, best online project?

- **Mass emails, newsletters, SMS, news forums**: Keep people up to date with the project. Give both the leaders and the users a clear and ongoing sense of project progress.

- **Formal training event**: Probably the best Big Bomb Tactic of all? Bring in internal or external experts (for example, from a Mahara partner) to run a few day courses, which will really get cohorts of users confidently up and running with your platform.

Situational Response Tactic 2: Sniper Fire

Sometimes there will be particular people who you will need to influence in order to affect change. Some people will have more charisma, more interpersonal skills than others and it will be these people who you will need to win over if you are going to encourage your people to adopt your platform. These people may not always be the people with the most important jobs, by the way! A secretary can often exert more influence than another manager, or a student in the class can often exert more influence over group behavior than the teacher.

- **Corridor conversations**: Identify an influential person and chat with them informally about the Mahara implementation (this can be a highly useful tactic).

- **Mentor matching**: Get Mahara adopters into situations (you may have to do this subtly and covertly) where they can enthuse about their Mahara use with people who are Mahara-reticent.

- **Targeted emails/SMS messages/phone calls**: Find your slow adopters and make them feel missed, make them feel identified, make them feel encouraged, and don't let up too quickly on encouraging them, there are all sorts of reasons why people may not feel involved.

- **Targeted feedback questionnaires and response strategy**: If you can identify the different types of change resisters (discussed previously) in a survey (be careful not to be too crass about it!), you can conduct a more targeted communication response to these different types of needs and resisters.

Evaluation and continuation

Once your platform is running, it's tempting to sit back, but you will need to think about what you are going to do next to ensure its continual development.

Reviewing and re-evaluating

This is one of those things that is much more easier said than done. It can be really hard to step back and take an honestly critical look at a platform that has been put in place.

Here are some questions you could be asking:

- Are the people we *need* to be recording their knowledge in Mahara actually recording their knowledge in Mahara? If not, why not? How can we make it happen?
- Is Mahara helping learners to achieve their qualifications? Is Mahara helping people to do their work?
- Can you offer *targeted* support for groups who have been slow to engage?
- Does *everything* really have to be digital?
- Are people actually identifying and meeting their learning, career, and personal goals?
- Is learning over Mahara ever being delivered more effectively through other online or offline approaches?
- Are there variations in success between different types of learners? Are there any good reasons for the variations? How should we respond to these variations?
- Do the groups, forums, or learning program briefs always match the aspirations and needs of the learners?
- Could you yourself set performance improvement targets based on metrics gathered from the sorts of questions we have just asked?
- Are achievement targets set for all courses at all levels?
- Is Mahara participation a requirement? Should it be a requirement? Should you set participation targets or might that have a negative effect?
- If any targets are set, is everyone made aware of those targets? How? How effectively?
- Are staff or users themselves involved in the target setting?
- How do you communicate progress against targets? (Simple graphical displays?)
- How do you celebrate and reward individual success and collective progress against targets?
- Are targets revised frequently enough? By whom? How ambitiously?
- Do we care about all these targets? Wouldn't it be best to leave the whole Mahara thing to grow ad hoc?

Changing and embedding

How are you going to make your Mahara ePortfolio site stick as one of the cornerstones of your learning delivery model? Or has it all been a flash in the pan?

A thriving site will often be in a constant state of flux, changing with the needs and focuses of the organization and its people, embedding itself deeper and deeper as an element of the wider e-institution.

There are various ways you might have approached the change-management process required to implement Mahara usage in your organization.

Some organizations might take a very top-down, **directive** sort of approach. The wisest among those avoid horrific staff rebellion by putting their weight behind an expert who is brought in to make the change happen. This expert is often a consultant, sometimes a new staff member. The **expert** will follow a strict project plan and will have the authority to reward and rebuke as deemed appropriate by the implementation planners.

Other organizations might adopt a more bottom-up **user-driven** sort of approach. They implement the platform, publicize it, and then just wait to see what happens. The problem here is that it can result in pretty much nothing getting done. It is therefore best, in this approach to encourage a **knowledge-sharing** culture. You could for example give the end users dedicated time to show off their work to each other and share their skills. This nudges progress along a bit without having to bring in an expert because the users are learning from each other.

In our view, an approach that sits in the middle of these two positions is best: a **negotiated**, circular approach, which not only clearly communicates the organizational drivers, but also gives ample space for the user community themselves to take the lead on what their learning content should cover. The Mahara platform itself, of course, allows nicely for this approach.

If you really want to change your learning and knowledge culture into a reflective, online ePortfolio, supported learning and knowledge culture, you will probably have to continuously re-evaluate to what extent you wish to **embed** Mahara use into your organizational policies. Here are the key questions:

- ◆ Is Mahara usage going to be integral to your business development plan? (This is the information age after all, and your country may even be a knowledge-based economy like the UK and USA?)
- ◆ Will Mahara usage be integral to your organizational policies and procedures?
- ◆ Will staff responsibilities for Mahara usage and management be a defined and remunerated element of their job descriptions? Or would you prefer to leave Mahara to be a self-managing phenomena?

B

Installing Mahara

This book is aimed at Mahara users, rather than Mahara administrators. However, a new user may wish to install a Mahara instance in order to experiment. Also, lots of people like to install Mahara on their own Linux machines or on a web server of their own in order to organize their own personal learning data.

This section is for those of you who have some knowledge of web applications and servers or feel that you could have a good go at installing Mahara.

Don't worry, we will keep it as simple as possible...

What will you need?

Before you can install Mahara, you will need to have access to a Linux server. It may be that you run Linux on a laptop or desktop at home or that your company or institution has its own Linux servers, in which case, great! If not, there are many hosting services available on the Internet, which will enable you to access a Linux server and therefore run Mahara.

It is important that you get a server to which you have **root** access. It is also important that you set your server up with the following features:

- ◆ **Database**: Mahara must have a database to work. The databases supported are PostgreSQL Version 8.1 or later and MySQL Version 5.0.25 or later. The Mahara developers recommend that you use PostgreSQL, if possible, but for most installations, MySQL will work just as well.
- ◆ **PHP**: Mahara requires PHP Version 5.1.3 or later.

♦ **Web Server**: The preferred web server is Apache.

♦ **PHP extensions**:

  ❏ **Compulsory Extensions**: GD, JSON, cURL, libxml, SimpleXML, Session, pgSQL or Mysqli, EXIF, OpenSSL or XML-RCP (for networking support)

  ❏ **Optional Extension**: Imagick

Ask your resident IT expert about the features listed above if you don't understand what they mean.

 A quick way to install some of the software listed above is to use the `apt-get install` command if you are using the Ubuntu/Debian Linux systems. See `http://www.debian.org/doc/manuals/apt-howto/` to find out more.

Downloading Mahara

It's time for action. Let's start by seeing how easy it is for us to get a copy of Mahara for ourselves, and the best part is... it's free!

Time for action – downloading Mahara

1. Go to `http://mahara.org`. Click on the **download** button on the Mahara home page. The button will be labeled with the name of the current version of Mahara:

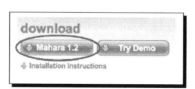

2. You will now see a web page that lists all the various versions of Mahara, both previous and forthcoming versions, in Alpha and Beta. Choose the most recent version from the list in the format you prefer. We recommend that you use the `.tar.gz` type because it is faster to download than `.zip`.

```
1.2.2 release from the 1.2 series released 2009-12-08
▷Release information
```

File	Description	Downloads
⬦ **mahara-1.2.2.zip** (md5, sig)	Mahara 1.2.2	1,671 last downloaded today
⬦ **mahara-1.2.2.tar.gz** (md5, sig)	Mahara 1.2.2	420 last downloaded today
⬦ **mahara-1.2.2.tar.bz2** (md5, sig)	Mahara 1.2.2	142 last downloaded 24 hours ago

4. You will be asked if you would like to open or save the file. Select **Save File**, and click **OK**.

5. That's all there is to it. Go to your Internet downloads folder. In there, you should see your newly downloaded Mahara package.

What Just Happened?

You have just taken your first step on the road to installing Mahara. We have seen the website we have to go to for downloading the most recent version and learned how to download the package in the format we prefer.

Using the command line

The best way of installing and administering your Mahara is to use the command line. This is a way of writing text commands to perform specific tasks, rather than having to use a graphical user interface. There are many things you can do from the command line, from common tasks such as copying and deleting files to more advanced ones such as downloading and installing software from the Internet.

A lot of the things we will be doing in this section assume that you will have Secure Shell Access to your server through the terminal command line.

If you have a Linux or a Mac computer, you can use the terminal on your machine to SSH into your web server. Windows users can achieve the same functionality by downloading a free terminal client called PuTTY from `http://www.chiark.greenend.org.uk/~sgtatham/putty/download.html`. Speak to your resident IT expert for more information on how to use the terminal, or see `http://www.physics.ubc.ca/mbelab/computer/linux-intro/html/` for an introduction to the Linux command line.

For now, let's just learn how to get the contents of our downloaded package into the correct place on our server.

Time for action – creating your Mahara file structure

1. Copy the `mahara-1.2.0.tar.gz` package you downloaded into your home directory on your web server. If you are copying the file to the server from your own computer, you can do this using the `scp` command (on Linux or Mac):

```
scp mahara-1.2.0.tar.gz servername:pathtohomedirectory
```

On Windows, you may prefer to use a free FTP utility such as FileZilla (`http://filezilla-project.org/`).

2. Unpack the contents of the Mahara package on the Linux server. On the terminal, you can do this using the `tar` command:

```
tar xvzf mahara-1.2.0.tar.gz
```

3. You will now see a new folder called `mahara-1.2.0`; you will need to rename this to `public`. To do this on the terminal, you can use the `mv` command:

```
mv mahara-1.2.0 public
```

4. That's it! The Mahara code is now in place.

What Just Happened?

You just learned where to copy the Mahara package on your server and how to extract its contents.

Creating the database

A lot of the information created in your Mahara will be stored in a database. Mahara offers support for both PostgreSQL and MySQL databases. However we prefer to use PostgreSQL. If you are interested, see `http://mahara.org/interaction/forum/topic.php?id=302` for a discussion on why PostgreSQL is preferred to MySQL.

The way you create your database will depend on who you have chosen to host your Mahara. Sometimes, your web host will provide a graphical user interface to access your server database. Get in touch with your local IT expert to find out how to do this.

However, for smaller Mahara installations, we often prefer to use something like phpPgAdmin, which is a software application that allows you to manage PostgreSQL databases over the Internet. See `http://phppgadmin.sourceforge.net` for more information on setting up phpPgAdmin on your server.

Also see `http://www.phpmyadmin.net/`, for phpMyAdmin which works in a very similar way to phpPgAdmin but operates on a MySQL database.

For now, let's get on with creating a Postgres database using our phpPgAdmin panel.

Time for action – creating the Mahara database

1. Open up your phpPgAdmin panel from your Internet browser and log in. The username is hopefully **postgres**. Contact your admin if you are unsure of the database password or how to locate the phyPgAdmin panel.

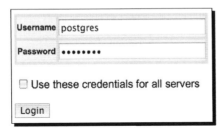

2. On the front page there is a section that invites you to **create database**, click there. Give your database a relevant name such as mysite_Mahara. Make sure you select the UTF8 collation from the drop-down box. Finally, click **Create**.

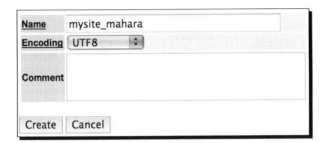

3. If you want to, it is a good idea to have a new user for each database you create. Use phpPgAdmin to create a new user.

4. That's it, you're done!

What Just Happened?

We just created the database for our Mahara installation using the open source phpPgAdmin tool available for Linux. Another way to create the database on your server is to use the database command line tool.

Have a go hero – using the command line to create your database

Using the command line is a much more elegant way to create the database and quicker once you get the hang of it. Why not have a go at creating the database using the command line? For instructions on how to do this see the database section of the Mahara installation guide: `http://wiki.mahara.org/System_Administrator%27s_Guide/Installing_Mahara`.

Setting up the data directory

Most of the data that is created in your Mahara is stored in the database. However, all the files that are uploaded by your users, such as their personal photos or documents, need to be stored in a separate place. This is where the data directory comes in.

The data directory is simply a folder that holds all of the "stuff" belonging to your users. Everything is kept safe by the data directory being outside of the home directory. This set up also makes it easy for you to migrate your Mahara to another server at some point in the future.

 The data directory is often referred to as the `dataroot`.

Time for action – setting up the data directory

1. Create the data directory in the `public` folder of your home directory. We will create the directory using the `mkdir` command and call it `uploaddir`:

   ```
   mkdir uploaddir
   ```

    It doesn't really matter what you decide to call your `dataroot` directory, but try to choose a name that is relevant to what the directory is doing. The name suggested by Mahara and the most commonly used name is `uploaddir`, but other names such as `maharadata` would be just as good.

2. Set the permissions on this folder using the `chmod` command:

   ```
   chmod -R 0777 uploaddir
   ```

3. Change the user of the new directory to be the same as your server using the `chown` command. The user is usually apache or www-data:

   ```
   chown -R www-data:www-data uploaddir
   ```

4. And that's all there is to it, we now have a place where Mahara can put all of the stuff belonging to our users.

What just happened?

What we have just done is really very simple, so hopefully you aren't feeling bogged down with all those commands you had to type.

We created our data directory and made sure that it was in a safe place in your home directory above the `htdocs` directory. Then we changed the permissions, users, and groups for the directory to make it easy for Mahara to put things in and to delete things.

Let's take a quick look at the file structure that we have just created for our Mahara installation:

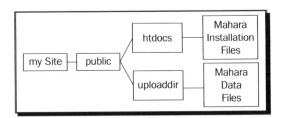

So far we have downloaded and put the Mahara files into place on our server and seen how to create the database and `dataroot` needed to store all the Mahara information.

Now, we have to hold Mahara's hand by letting it know how it can access the database and how to find the `dataroot`. To do this we use an important file called `config.php`.

Time for action – creating the config.php file

1. In the `htdocs` folder of your Mahara site you will find a file called `config-dist.php`. Use the `nano` command in your terminal to start editing `config-dist.php` file.

```
nano config-dist.php
```

 Other Linux people use much more sophisticated text editors like Vim (`http://www.vim.org/`) and Emacs (`http://www.gnu.org/software/emacs/`). We are simple folk and are perfectly happy with nano: `http://www.nano-editor.org/`.

2. You will now see the file open on the command line. Use the arrow keys on your keyboard to scroll up and down the page until you get to a section called **database connection details**. In the following example the user is using `mysql5`, rather than PostgreSQL. Fill in the information so that it matches the details you used to set up your own database:

```
// database connection details
// valid values for dbtype are 'postgres8' and 'mysql5'
$cfg->dbtype    = 'mysql5';
$cfg->dbhost    = 'localhost';
$cfg->dbport    = null;
$cfg->dbname    = 'mysite_mahara';
$cfg->dbuser    = 'mysite';
$cfg->dbpass    = 'sharing';
```

3. Next, continue scrolling down the file until you reach a line that starts with `$cfg->dataroot`. Here, you must fill in the full path from the server root directory to the data directory we created earlier in this chapter.

```
// This path must be writable by the webserver and outside document root (the
// place where the Mahara files like index.php have been installed).
// Mahara will NOT RUN if this is inside your document root, because
// this is a big security hole.
$cfg->dataroot = '/srv/mysite.tdm.info/public/uploaddir';
```

4. Congratulations, you've now finished editing the configuration file. Save it by clicking *Ctrl + C* on your keyboard. When asked if you would like to rename the file, type **Y** for yes and name the file `config.php`.

What Just Happened?

What we just did was very important, we let Mahara know where the database is and the password needed to access it. We also let it know the location of the `dataroot` directory.

Running the Installer

Now that we've done all the hard work it's time to let the Mahara installer do its magic. The main job that the installer does is to add new tables to the database that we created earlier.

Time for action – running the installer

1. The Mahara installer is started when you navigate to the `wwwroot` (the location you have installed Mahara) in your Internet browser. For example, we visit `http://mysite.tdm.info`. Your domain will have a different name.

2. The first page you see in the installer invites you to read the GNU General Public License. Click **I agree** to continue.

If you don't see the GNU information screen, then it is likely that you have done something wrong. Mahara will typically give you a message at this point explaining what the problem is.

3. The next page is where all the important work is being done. You will see each component being installed in the database. If everything goes well, the information section on the right-hand side should have a green check mark for each component. When the installation has finished, click **Continue** at the bottom of the page.

4. And that's all there is to it! You will now see the home page of your very own Mahara, and I'm sure you can't wait to log in for the first time.

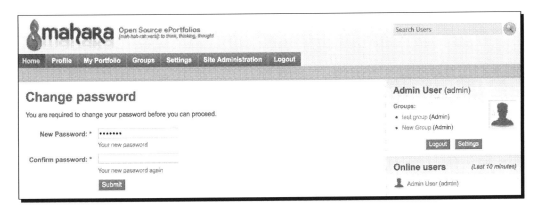

The last step: Setting up a cron process

Before you can be let loose on your Mahara, there is one last thing that you must remember to do to complete the installation: set up a cron job. If, like me, when I installed Mahara for the first time, you are thinking "What on earth is a cron job?", don't worry, it is relatively simple.

The cron job is a process that simply enables a number of tasks to be performed regularly, typically every hour. This is useful for updating RSS feeds, amongst other things. The easiest way to add a cron process on a Debian or Ubuntu Linux server is to add a new entry in a file, called a `crontab`, by using the command:

```
crontab -e
```

...and adding a line similar to:

```
* * * * www-data php /path/to/mahara/htdocs/lib/cron.php
```

If you are interested, see `http://www.adminschoice.com/docs/crontab.htm` for more information on `crontab` files.

Can I install Mahara on Windows?

At the moment, the Mahara developers offer no support for running Mahara on Windows Servers. It is designed to primarily work with Linux, Apache, PHP, and open source SQL databases.

This, however, doesn't mean that Mahara won't work on Windows, so If you are feeling adventurous why not give it a go and report back to Mahara on your experience?

What about installation on other operating systems?

The Mahara developers state clearly that they don't test their system with any other operating systems, including Solaris, Mac, and BSD. Again, that isn't to say that Mahara won't work on these systems, it is just best if you play it safe and choose to run your Mahara on the system that it was built for—Linux.

What is a Mahara partner and what can they do for me?

Most people using a tool like Mahara for the first time will shudder at the thought of doing an installation on a Linux server. In fact, "What is Linux?" is the most likely response. If this is you, then there are people who can help you out!

Mahara partners are specialists who know how to:

♦ Install Mahara on a server

♦ Host your Mahara

♦ Offer support for developing your Mahara in the future

♦ Upgrade your Mahara when new versions come out

♦ Theme your Mahara

- ◆ Provide training
- ◆ Provide implementation consultancy support
- ◆ ...and more!

Mahara partners have a special relationship with the Mahara developer team and are very knowledgeable about how Mahara works. They can do all the things you don't feel comfortable doing, or don't want to do, such as installing your Mahara, hosting it on the Internet, and managing it. This will be at a cost and will depend on the individual partner.

Even if you do have confidence that you could install Mahara on a Linux server, it is still very likely that a Mahara partner has something to offer you. For example, you might want to brighten up the look of your Mahara to match your corporate branding but have no knowledge of internet technologies such as CSS and (X)HTML.

So where can you find out more about Mahara partners?

Finding a Mahara partner

The easiest way to find a Mahara Partner is to visit the **Partners** section of the Mahara website. See `http://mahara.org/partners`. This will open a page listing all the Mahara partners. If you are thinking about using a Mahara partner, have a look through the description of the services that each one offers and decide whether they are right for you. Each partner also has a website that you can visit to find out more information. The Mahara partners are based all over the world, so it is a good idea to find one that is close to wherever you are.

C

Pop Quiz Answers

Chapter 2

Understanding your profile information

1	5 Icons.
2	Goals.

Chapter 3

files, folders, and tagging

1	Tags.
2	You could structure your folder by file type, audience, topic, reference code, or any other structure that is useful for you.
3	Yes.
4	Your site administrator.

blogging in Mahara

1	You can use your blog for both these purposes, and more. You may also want to use it to record your simple factual information at certain times. For example, you could bullet-point a few key learning points following each lesson in your blog. These can then be used as part of a revision program for an exam.
2	You can use your blog for both these purposes, and more.

Chapter 4

Creating a View

1	The Wall block.
2	The overriding time removes any individual access times that you have set.
3	This is a difficult to guess URL generated by Mahara which can be sent to people outside the Mahara site to give them access to your View.
4	You can set access to as many groups or individuals as you wish.
5	Yes, you can go back and edit your View access as many times as you wish.

Copying Views

1	Normally it will be called 'Copy of (View name)', but the user who copied it may have renamed it.
2	The View access rights aren't copied when you copy a View. Also depending on how the other user has set up permissions, not all artifacts are always copied, for example, you may find that some blogs or files haven't been copied.

Chapter 5

Creating Mahara Groups

1	Anybody in the Mahara site can join an open membership group.
2	By making your group publicly viewable, you are allowing people outside of Mahara to view and access materials in your group without being logged in.
3	A Group Administrator can manage group members, create forums, edit, and delete forum posts of other users and edit group settings.

Group Forums

1	Moderators can edit or delete topics / posts in your forum. They should be responsible for checking that users in the forum are following some standard guidelines for behavior.
2	A Sticky topic is one that stays at the topic of a forum so that it is the first or one of the first that users see.
3	It is best to name your forums generally. Topics should relate to a more specific issue within the forum. It should be clear in a topic title what is being discussed.

Chapter 6

Activity Types

1	1
2	4
3	7
4	5
5	2
6	3
7	6

Export

1	LEAP2A

Chapter 7

Managing an Institution

1	A CSV file.
2	**Any 3 from:** They can respond to request to join the institution, invite members to join the institution, add users, suspend users, delete users, make users into Institutional Staff Members, and make users into Institutional Administrators.
3	Disallows users from logging in.

Index

A

activity preferences, Mahara
  about 152
  notification types 152
  selecting 153-156
admin notifications, Mahara site
  dealing with 178, 179
aesthetics section, View quality checklist
about 103
analysis and specification phase, Mahara imple-
    mentation
  about 202
  adapting 205
  administrating 205
  commitment, ensuring 210
  data, collecting 205
  data, organizing 205
  data, selecting 205
  implementation plan, scoping out 209
  implementation timeframe, deciding 210
  implementing 205
  initial Mahara design, drafting out 210, 211
  Mahara, embedding 213
  Mahara-specific policies, drafting out 212, 213
  planning 205
  publishing 205
  reflecting 205
  representing 205
  specific needs 206, 207
  testing 205
  threshold concepts 208
  usability 205
  verifying 205
  working conditions 206, 207
assessment manager 197

assessment page 197
assessment process, Mahara
  about 193
  example 195-198

B

blocks 90
blocks, group views
  adding 133
blog 62
blogging 62

C

closed topic, forum discussion frameworks 128
collaborative learning, Mahara
  about 18
  course groups 18
  friends, making 18
  Moodle, integrating with 18
  working and learning, in groups 18
config.php file
  creating 227, 228
content section, View quality checklist 104, 105
Controlled membership group
  about 112, 183
  setting up 185, 186
course group, Mahara
  about 112, 182
  case study 185
  controlled membership groups 183
  request membership groups 183
  setting up 189
cron job 230
cron process, Mahara
  setting up 229, 230

D

data directory, Mahara
  about 226
  setting up 226
design and implementation phase, Mahara
       implementation
  about 213
  buzz, creating 213
  implementation resistors 216
  quick wins 214
  situational response tactics 216, 217
  users, involving in design process 215

E

e-portfolios
  about 8, 9
  features 19, 20
evaluation and continuation phase, Mahara
       implementation
  about 217
  changing 219
  embedding 219
  re-evaluating 218
  reviewing 218
examples, Mahara
  group of friends 9
  group of professionals 10
  large organization 10
  private training provider 9
  professional body 9
  recruitment agency 9
  school teacher 9
  student union 9
  university or college 9

F

footer, Mahara 33
forum discussion frameworks
  about 125
  choosing candidates 125
  closed topic 128
  combining versions 125
  comparing 125
  detecting differences 125
  discussion topic, adding 126-128
  ideas from central theme 125
  implications 125
  interpretations 125
  layout problems 125
  planning projects 125
  putting in order 125
  question and answer 125
  sticky topic 128
  surveys of opinion 125
forums
  about 119
  creating 120-122
  managing 123, 124
  moderating 122, 123
  naming 129
  topic post, replying to 130, 131
  topic, posting 129
  topics 124
friend request
  responding 140
friends
  adding, to list 139
  filtering 140, 141
  finding 139
  making 138
  managing 140
  removing 140, 141

G

Group Administrator 118
group files 132
group forums 119
group members
  about 118
  managing 116
  removing 116-118
  roles, changing 116-118
group views
  about 133, 134
  blocks 133
  RSS feeds, adding 133
  text box, adding 133
groups shortcut sideblock 114
groups, Mahara 107

H

HTML export, portfolio 160

I

Inchworms 24
institution, Mahara site
  about 164
  administering 165
  admin notifications, dealing with 178, 179
  example 164
  managing 181
  member roles, managing 175, 176
  settings, configuring 177, 178
  users, adding 166-169
  users, bulk uploading 169
institution administrator, Mahara site
  about 165
  responsibilities 165
institutional user account settings, Mahara site
  about 171
  editing 171
  institution settings 172
  site account settings 171
  suspend/delete user settings 171
  user, finding 172
  user, suspending 172
institutional users, Mahara site
  account settings, editing 171
  adding, CSV used 169, 170
institution files, Mahara 180
institution member, Mahara site
  managing 175, 176
institution views, Mahara 179, 180
invite only group
  about 111, 112
  creating 111, 112

J

Janet Norman from Pharmaceuticals Interna-
    tional Inc. case study 11, 12

L

LEAP2A export, portfolio 160
learner-driven aspects, Mahara 181

M

Mahara
  about 7
  activity preferences 152
  assessment process 193
  blocks 90
  blog 62
  blogging 62
  collaborative learning 18
  community, joining 20
  course group 182
  cron process, setting up 229, 230
  downloading 222, 223
  example assessment process 195-198
  features 15, 202-204
  folder structure, modifying 56
  institution 164
  institutional theming 164
  Janet Norman from Pharmaceuticals Interna-
      tional Inc. case study 11, 12
  learner-driven aspects 181
  main menu 32
  profile, setting up 33
  submenus 32
  Neil from Training 4 Work case study 13
  notifications 148
  personalized learning 16
  portfolio, exporting 157, 159
  preferences, in right sidebar 148
  Publicly Viewable groups 186, 187
  Punam from Pennytown Primary case study 10,
      11
  reflective learning 17
  site preferences 144
  staff members 182
  tutors 187
  used, as USB-Stick 53, 54
  Views 73
  watchlist 152
  ways, of using 9, 10
  website 24
  work, submitting for assessment 190
Mahara blog
  about 62
  creating 63-65
  image, embedding 66-68

Mahara community
  about 20
  joining 20
  registering 22, 23
Mahara database
  creating 224, 225
  creating, command line used 226
Mahara files
  copyright 56
  deleting 57
  folder structure, modifying 56
  moving 57
  multiple files, uploading 58, 59
  organizing, tags used 59-61
  upload limit 57
Mahara file structure
  creating 224
Mahara group
  about 107
  creating 108-110
  discussion forums, configuring 108
  forum discussion frameworks 125
  forum moderation 122
  forum topics 124
  forums 119
  forums, managing 123, 124
  forums, naming 129
  friend request, responding 140
  friends, making 138
  friends, managing 140
  group files 132, 133
  group files, sharing 108
  group members, managing 116
  group views 133
  group views, creating 108
  groups shortcut sideblock 114
  groups, finding 136
  groups, joining 135, 136
  invite only groups 111
  navigating 112, 113
  open membership group, joining 115
  open membership groups 110
  relationships 183
  request membership group, joining 136, 137
  request membership groups 111

  request, accepting/denying 138
  topic, posting on forum 129
  types 110
Mahara implementation
  about 201
  analysis and specification phase 201, 202
  design and implementation phase 202, 213
  evaluation and continuation 202
  evaluation and continuation phase 217
Mahara installation
  pre-requisites 221
Mahara installer
  running 228, 229
Mahara partners
  about 24, 230, 231
  searching 231
Mahara site
  another user, masquerading 173, 174
  logging in 30, 31
  profile page 41
  registering with 27-29
Mahara themes 31
Mahara's user interface 31
Mahara, as USB-Stick
  about 53, 54
  files and folders, adding to portfolio 54-56
multi-page view
  creating 100-102

N

Neil from Training 4 Work case study 13
notifications, Mahara
  about 148
  managing 149-152

O

open membership group
  about 110
  creating 110
  joining 115
  maharaforbeginners.tdm.info, joining 115

P

personalized learning, Mahara
  about 16
  access control 17
  accessible 16
  personalized self-presentation 16
  privacy 16
  transfer your data 16
portfolio, Mahara
  exporting 157, 159
  HTML export 160
  LEAP2A 157
  LEAP2A export 160
  Standalone HTML website 157
profile icons, Mahara site
  about 36
  uploading 37
profile, Mahara site
  editing 34-36
  profile icons 36
  profile icons, uploading 37
  profile information 34
  resume goals and skills, editing 39, 40
  setting up 33
profile page, Mahara site
  about 41
  blogs, linking to 68-70
  examples 43, 44
  files, linking to 68-70
  folders, linking to 68-70
  investigating 41, 43
  profile page wall 43
  text box, adding 44
  text box, creating 45, 46
  viewing 41, 43
profile page wall, Mahara site 43
Publicly Viewable groups 186, 187
Punam from Pennytown Primary case study 10, 11

Q

quality checklist, Views
  aesthetics section 103, 104
  content section 104, 105

R

real-life Maharas 14, 15
reflective learning, Mahara
  about 17
  blogs, keeping 17
  goals and skills, developing 17
  other platforms, integrating with 17
request membership group
  about 111, 183
  creating 111
  joining 136, 137
resume goals and skills, Mahara site
  editing 38-40

S

secret URLs 197
site blocks, Mahara 33
site preferences, Mahara
  changing 144, 145
  controls, showing 147
  friends control 146
  HTML editor 146
  maximum cloud tags 148
  messaging options 146, 147
  password, changing 145
  username, changing 145
staff members, Mahara
  about 182
  institutional staff members 182
  site staff members 182
sticky topic, forum discussion frameworks 128

T

text box
  adding, to profile page 44, 45
  creating 45
  editing 48
  formatting 50
  hyperlink, adding 48, 49
  image, adding 51, 52
text editor, options 48
threshold concepts
  disruptive nature 209

learning activity design 208
ownership 209
processes 208
purpose 208
tutor
about 187
adding, to course group 188, 189

U

ULCC ILP 198
user interface, Mahara
about 31
footer 33
Mahara themes 31, 32
main menu 32
site blocks 33
submenus 32

V

Views, Mahara
about 73
access, controlling 86, 87
access, editing 83, 84

access time, setting 88
columns, adding/removing 79
copy-able View, making 85
copying 93-95
creating 75
details, adding 82
editing 89, 90
feedback 96-98
laying out 75-79
layout, changing 80, 81
multi-page view 99
multi-page view, making 100-102
quality, accessing 102
quality checklist 103
stages, of creation 74
uses 74

W

watchlist, Mahara 152
work submission
about 190
submitted view, releasing 192, 193
view, submitting for assessment 190, 191

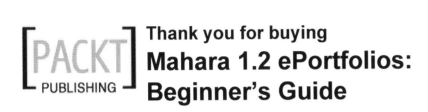

Thank you for buying
Mahara 1.2 ePortfolios: Beginner's Guide

Packt Open Source Project Royalties

When we sell a book written on an Open Source project, we pay a royalty directly to that project. Therefore by purchasing Mahara 1.2 ePortfolios: Beginner's Guide, Packt will have given some of the money received to the Mahara project.

In the long term, we see ourselves and you—customers and readers of our books—as part of the Open Source ecosystem, providing sustainable revenue for the projects we publish on. Our aim at Packt is to establish publishing royalties as an essential part of the service and support a business model that sustains Open Source.

If you're working with an Open Source project that you would like us to publish on, and subsequently pay royalties to, please get in touch with us.

Writing for Packt

We welcome all inquiries from people who are interested in authoring. Book proposals should be sent to author@packtpub.com. If your book idea is still at an early stage and you would like to discuss it first before writing a formal book proposal, contact us; one of our commissioning editors will get in touch with you.

We're not just looking for published authors; if you have strong technical skills but no writing experience, our experienced editors can help you develop a writing career, or simply get some additional reward for your expertise.

About Packt Publishing

Packt, pronounced 'packed', published its first book "Mastering phpMyAdmin for Effective MySQL Management" in April 2004 and subsequently continued to specialize in publishing highly focused books on specific technologies and solutions.

Our books and publications share the experiences of your fellow IT professionals in adapting and customizing today's systems, applications, and frameworks. Our solution-based books give you the knowledge and power to customize the software and technologies you're using to get the job done. Packt books are more specific and less general than the IT books you have seen in the past. Our unique business model allows us to bring you more focused information, giving you more of what you need to know, and less of what you don't.

Packt is a modern, yet unique publishing company, which focuses on producing quality, cutting-edge books for communities of developers, administrators, and newbies alike. For more information, please visit our website: www.PacktPub.com.

Moodle 1.9 for Teaching 7-14 Year Olds

Moodle 1.9 for Teaching 7-14 Year Olds

ISBN: 978-1-847197-14-6   Paperback: 236 pages

Effective e-learning for younger students using Moodle as your Classroom Assistant

1. Focus on the unique needs of young learners to create a fun, interesting, interactive, and informative learning environment your students will want to go on day after day

2. Engage and motivate your students with games, quizzes, movies, and podcasts the whole class can participate in

3. Go paperless! Put your lessons online and grade them anywhere, anytime

Moodle 1.9
E-Learning Course Development

Moodle 1.9 E-Learning Course Development

ISBN: 978-1-847193-53-7   Paperback: 360 pages

A complete guide to successful learning using Moodle

1. Updated for Moodle version 1.9

2. Straightforward coverage of installing and using the Moodle system

3. Working with Moodle features in all learning environments

4. A unique course-based approach focuses your attention on designing well-structured, interactive, and successful courses

Please check **www.PacktPub.com** for information on our titles

Moodle Course Conversion: Beginner's Guide

ISBN: 978-1-847195-24-1   Paperback: 294 pages

Taking existing classes online quickly with the Moodle LMS

1. No need to start from scratch! This book shows you the quickest way to start using Moodle and e-learning, by bringing your existing lesson materials into Moodle.

2. Move your existing course notes, worksheets, and resources into Moodle quickly then improve your course, taking advantage of multimedia and collaboration.

3. Moving marking online – no more backbreaking boxes of assignments to lug to and from school or college

Elgg Social Networking

ISBN: 978-1-847192-80-6   Paperback: 196 pages

Create and manage your own social network site using this free open-source tool

1. Create your own customized community site

2. Manage users, invite friends, start groups and blogs

3. Host content: photos, videos, MP3s, podcasts

4. Manage your Elgg site, protect it from spam

5. Written on Elgg version 0.9

Please check **www.PacktPub.com** for information on our titles

Moodle 1.9 Extension Development [RAW]

ISBN: 978-1-847194-24-4   Paperback: 310 pages

Customize and extend Moodle using its robust plug-in systems

1. Develop your own blocks, activities, filters, and organize your content with secure code

2. Thoroughly covers key libraries of Moodle and best practices to use them

3. Explore the Moodle architectural concepts, how it is structured, and how it works

4. Detailed examples and screenshots for easy learning

Moodle Administration

ISBN: 978-1-847195-62-3   Paperback: 376 pages

An administrator's guide to configuring, securing, customizing, and extending Moodle

1. A complete guide for planning, installing, optimizing, customizing, and configuring Moodle

2. Secure, back up, and restore your VLE

3. Extending and networking Moodle

4. Detailed walkthroughs and expert advice on best practices

5. Checklist of over 100 common problems with solutions

6. This book covers Moodle 1.9

Please check **www.PacktPub.com** for information on our titles

Moodle 1.9 Multimedia

ISBN: 978-1-847195-90-6   Paperback: 272 pages

Engaging online language learning activities using the Moodle platform

1. Ideas and best practices for teachers and trainers on using multimedia effectively in Moodle

2. Ample screenshots and clear explanations to facilitate learning

3. Covers working with TeacherTube, embedding interactive Flash games, podcasting, and more

4. Create instructional materials and design students' activities around multimedia

Moodle 1.9 Teaching Techniques

ISBN: 978-1-849510-06-6   Paperback: 216 pages

Creative ways to build powerful and effective online courses

1. Motivate students from all backgrounds, generations, and learning styles

2. When and how to apply the different learning solutions with workarounds, providing alternative solutions

3. Easy-to-follow, step-by-step instructions with screenshots and examples for Moodle's powerful features

4. Especially suitable for university and professional teachers

Please check **www.PacktPub.com** for information on our titles

Made in the USA
Lexington, KY
22 November 2010